The Art of
Meeting Women
A Guide for Gay Women

The Art of
Meeting Women

A Guide for Gay Women

Rhona Sacks

How to Meet the Women
You Want to Meet

SLOPE BOOKS™

PUBLISHER'S NOTE:
This book is designed to provide accurate and authoritative information in regard to the subject matter covered. It is sold with the understanding that neither the author nor the publisher is engaged in rendering psychological or other professional service.

The purpose of this book is to educate and entertain. The author does not dispense psychological advice or prescribe the use of any technique as a form of treatment for psychological problems without the advice of a mental health professional, either directly or indirectly. The intent of the author is only to offer information of a general nature to help you in your pursuit for emotional well-being. If you require psychological advice or other expert assistance, seek the services of a competent professional person.

The author and the publisher have neither liability nor responsibility to any person or entity with respect to any loss or damage caused, or alleged to be caused, directly or indirectly, by the information contained in this book. In the event you use any of the information in this book for yourself, which is your constitutional right, the author and the publisher assume no responsibility for your actions.

Published and distributed in the United States by:
SLOPE BOOKS™ Van Brunt Station P.O. Box 150636 Brooklyn, NY 11215-0636
For toll-free orders, call: (888) GAY WOMAN
Visit us on the internet at www.gaywoman.com

Publisher's Cataloging-in-Publication
(Provided by Quality Books, Inc.)
Sacks, Rhona
        The art of meeting women : a guide for gay women : how to
        meet the women you want to meet / Rhona Sacks. — 1st ed.
        p. cm.
        Includes index.
        Preassigned LCCN: 97-91117
        ISBN: 0-9660698-0-3
        1. Lesbians—Social networks. 2. Dating (Social customs) 3.
        Female friendship. I. Title.
HQ75.5.S33 1998   305.48'9664
                              QBI97-41297

Table of Contents

Acknowledgments

I wish to express my gratitude and love to the spectacular women and men who *patiently* supported me through the intensive process of creating this book.

I especially want to thank:

Elaine, Harold, and Marc Sacks—I couldn't ask for a more caring family. Thank you for everything. Laura Lee Baron—You're an extraordinary woman. Thank you for sharing your gifts with me. Lisa Cohen—Your talent is surpassed only by your kindness. Thank you for being such a wonderful friend. Patricia Ellis—Miss Patty, I am truly blessed by your friendship. Kisses and hugs and lots of love. Kathleen Mary Gallagher—You're an absolute joy in my life. I love you, sweetie. S. Blaine Martin— Many thanks for your beautiful work and friendship. Your generosity of spirit is deeply felt and appreciated. Cary Scott Siegel—You're a constant reminder of the magic that can occur when love eclipses fear. Thank you for the past twenty years. Orie Urami— Thank you for the gift of teaching me to trust from my heart and soul. I treasure our friendship, and I love you.

And, I want to thank the best kitty in the world, Simon, for being an endless source of joy.

Book design by Beyond the Desktop
Book cover by NiceMedia
Web site by TracerOne Business Services

To my wonderful lesbian family—
may we continue learning new ways
of loving ourselves and each other.

Introduction

*"To cheat oneself out of love is
the most terrible deception; it is
an eternal loss for which there is
no reparation, either in time or
in eternity."*
—Kierkegaard

A familiar social scene:

Two friends are at a dance club. One of them spots a woman and begins to breathe heavily. She points out the object of her affection to her friend:

"Hey, look at that woman. She's adorable. What a great smile!"

"Do you think she's with someone?"

"I don't think so."

"Why don't you go over and ask her to dance?"

"Oh, no, I couldn't do that. She's too cute; she probably has a girlfriend somewhere. What if I go over there, ask her to dance and she says, 'No'? Forget it. I'm gonna get a drink, you want one?"

There it goes—another missed opportunity to meet a woman, possibly a nice woman, perhaps a terrific woman, perchance *the* woman. But the amorous admirer in our story will never know. The chance to make contact with a new friend or lover is wasted. The moment is lost due to ... *fear*! This small word packs a big punch. Fear can consume us with insecurity and freeze us into inaction. It is the reason behind all of our aborted or botched attempts at meeting each other.

How often do you find yourself in a promising situation but choose to do nothing?

▼ You stay home instead of going to a party.

▼ Upon entering a crowded bar, you summarily conclude that every woman looks boring or bitchy and leave as quickly as possible.

▼ You decide not to say, *"Hi!"* to that interesting looking woman in the bookstore whom you notice noticing you.

▼ While in a dance club, you cling to old friends rather than asking someone new to dance.

Why do we behave this way?

Fear.

Even when we are isolated from and lonely for each other, we still can not reach out. What are we so afraid of? That's an easy question to answer: *rejection!* In social scrambles, every one of us struggles against this mighty foe.

Fear of rejection lurks within the questions many of us ask ourselves and our friends:

"Why am I sometimes shy?"

"Why is it more difficult to approach the woman I am the most interested in meeting?"

"Why can't I easily make eye contact with a woman I find attractive?"

"Why do I feel tense upon entering a room filled with strangers?"

"Why can't I walk up to a woman and introduce myself without experiencing anxiety?"

"Why am I apprehensive about joining a group of women I don't know?"

"Why can I never think of anything to say when I first meet a woman?"

"Why am I reluctant to ask a woman out on a date?"

"Why can't I find anyone I'm interested in dating?"

Like me, you've probably spent too many nights with your friends complaining about how hard it is not only to meet women, but to meet the women you want to meet. Perhaps, like me, you decided to seek out women-meeting information, searching the local libraries and bookstores—but all you could find were a few books listing lesbian bars and bookstores and many books offering guys tips for picking up girls. These books were no help in showing you ways to meet compatible gay women comfortably and easily.

When I finally exhausted all the outlets available for gay women, I realized there was only one solution: If no one was going to teach me how to do this, I was going to teach myself. I pretended I was an anthropology student with a fascinating research project: "Lesbian Meeting Habits." My mission was to find answers to two burning questions:

> *Why* is it so difficult for us to meet each other?
>
> *How* can we meet the women we want to meet confidently and easily?

I knew that if I didn't do something to find the answers to these questions—fast—I was probably going to end up living a very lonely lesbian life.

This book is the product of my exploration in asking questions, listening to answers, formulating ideas, soliciting opinions, observing lesbian meeting habits, learning from mistakes, and personally experiencing as much as possible. All in the name of research, of course. Hundreds of gay women from all over the country generously shared their time and honesty about themselves and their meeting habits.

Some of my friends have declared this project a thinly-veiled excuse for me to meet more women. I have savvy friends. In fact, that wasn't my reason for writing this—or at least not my main one. I wanted to share my philosophy and strategies on how to meet other gay women for one reason—to increase the amount of love we have for ourselves and for each other.

We live in a highly homophobic world, one whose unrelenting verbal and sometimes physical attacks can destroy even the strongest woman's self-esteem. The only balm that can soothe the pain of living in such a hostile and unaccepting environment is love—especially the love of our beautiful, diverse lesbian community.

We want to meet other gay women for obvious reasons: friendship and romance. Unfortunately, we aren't always sure how to do it. We are social creatures by nature, but we don't come with instructions as to how to make contact with each other effectively.

Whenever someone asks me to describe the best way to meet women, I simply say, *"Be your best self."* What I mean by being your *best* self is being your *loving* self, that part of you which is confident, sincere, and caring. When you are able to reach out to women from this place, your fear of being rejected is greatly decreased, and your ability to connect successfully is dramatically increased. The techniques offered in this book will help you to tap that most resourceful, and most powerful, part of yourself.

Before we can journey outward and lovingly connect with other women, we must first journey inward and lovingly connect with ourselves. I hope this book will provide helpful insight into why we struggle to make contact with other gay women, and the psychological and practical tools with which to go out and meet, greet, and bond with each other.

If you are both persistent and patient in using the suggestions and methods I outline in the following pages, you will be amazed at the high level of self-confidence you can achieve in all areas of your life.

The essence of this book is *love*, as love is the pathway not only to a joyous and fulfilling social life, but to a joyous and fulfilling life.

Writing this book turned out to be a journey toward a deeper understanding of myself. I hope that reading it will prove to be as rewarding and successful a pilgrimage of *self-discovery* for you.

Part One

The Inner World

*"Make not your thoughts
your prisons."*
—Shakespeare

Chapter One

Social Insecurity

*"Fear is the darkness where
negatives are developed."*
—Anonymous

"Whenever I walk into a crowded room of women, my heart pounds, my hands sweat, and my stomach clenches. I don't know why I feel so nervous. All I know is that I always feel this way. Approaching a woman I don't know is unthinkable."

"I have a hard time meeting women who interest me. My pattern is to go to an event, take a look around, decide every woman there isn't for me, and leave after thirty minutes."

"I find going to a club or bar is really uncomfortable. And that's when I go with friends. Going alone is even worse. Once I went to a lesbian bar by myself; no one talked to me. I drank a couple of beers, and I left after an hour. It was the pits."

Do these scenes seem familiar to you?

Most of us have walked into a room filled with strangers and felt the same way. When I first started dating women, I noticed how difficult it was for gay women (including myself) to be assertive about meeting each other. It surprised me how many of us were infected with a devastating disorder, social insecurity. This dastardly disease strikes without warning, rendering normally intelligent women paralyzed and mute whenever they want to approach a stranger and strike up a conversation.

In an effort to understand the origins of social insecurity, I began to study the interaction (or lack thereof) of gay women with each other. Lesbian clubs and bars were my first stop, as they seemed to be one of the most difficult places to meet women. I instantly detected a disturbing trend: the remarkable number of women standing against the wall, looking nervous and uncomfortable.

I observed women looking at each other, but only for a second or two. Occasionally, a woman would turn to her friend and whisper something, nod in the direction of some woman, smile, perhaps laugh, and then ... do nothing. She would continue standing there, playing with her drink, and talking to her friend. There would be no attempt to make contact with the woman being admired. This is how the rest of the night, the rest of many nights, is typically played out for many gay women.

What could be the reason for such behavior? What causes those glue-traps on the bottom of our shoes, which stop us from walking toward a woman we want to meet, and those dust-mites in our throats, which keep us from introducing ourselves? The answer to both of these questions is, of course, *fear of rejection*.

Fear of rejection, the primary obstacle to successful meeting and greeting, is the anxiety of being disapproved of or disliked; the worry about being ignored, embarrassed, or humiliated; and the dread of being subjected to criticism or disrespect. Fear of rejection is the terror of hearing the word, *"No."* It causes our palms to sweat, our stomach to tie in knots, and our hearts to pound!

When we fear rejection, we procrastinate, rationalize, blame, criticize, complain, and judge. We refuse to be emotionally open, we remain in dissatisfying relationships, and we do not reach out to each other. Fear of rejection impairs our ability to take control of our lives. In effect, we stay stuck.

WHAT CAUSES FEAR OF REJECTION?

As children, we are taught the ways we have to behave to ensure that the significant people in our lives continue to love and approve of us. What these lessons teach us is not how to be our true selves but rather how to show those parts of ourselves that will be rewarded with approval—training in "conditional" love. As we grow up, how other people see and judge us becomes more and more important to our own self-esteem. We begin to disown our true selves in an effort to be liked and accepted. The seeds of self-denial make a fertile ground in which fear of rejection can grow and flourish.

The emotion of fear of rejection is born of the belief, *"If a woman turns me down, I am unworthy."* Underlying the emotion is the thought, *"If a woman is not interested in me, I am not good enough."*

SELF-ESTEEM AND FEAR OF REJECTION

Self-esteem and fear of rejection are inextricably linked. The monster of fear of rejection is only able to sink its teeth into us when our self-esteem is low. A woman with low self-esteem shies away from other women because her primary motivation is to avoid pain (rejection). She fears rejection because she believes other women determine her self-worth. If a woman rejects her, she rejects herself.

The pain of fear of rejection is invariably relieved by the salve of a healthy self-esteem. A woman with high self-esteem approaches other women to gain pleasure, to make contact. She doesn't fear possible rejection because the reactions of others don't dictate her own sense of self; she doesn't look to others to define who she is. A woman with a healthy self-esteem has nothing to fear because she believes she is a woman of worth, *independent* of how others see her.

Like many psychological terms, there is no one commonly accepted definition of self-esteem. I offer my own: Self-esteem is how much you love yourself. Loving yourself is not narcissism or egomania; these spring from emotional insecurity rather than security, from the fear that one is not good enough. Nor is self-love arrogance. Arrogance stems from an absence of self-love, not an abundance of it.

Loving yourself is *honoring* and *nurturing* the self; it involves taking good care of yourself. When you act from love, you are in the ideal emotional position to meet and create fulfilling relationships with other women.

WHERE DOES LOW SELF-ESTEEM COME FROM?

Self-esteem is not inborn; we learn it. Do we learn low self-esteem from growing up in a dysfunctional family, from living in a stifling society which pummels us with self-hating religious and cultural messages? Probably. I don't know precisely where each of us learned our individual lessons of not caring for and appreciating the self. What I do know is that the path to a better sense of self begins with the recognition that our self-esteem is, in fact, wounded. Once we acknowledge this, we can search for ways in which to *heal* it.

Chapter Two

Self-Esteem

*"We are what we think; all that
we are arises with our thoughts.
With our thoughts, we
make our world."*
—Buddha

This chapter contains potent concepts to aid you in strengthening your self-esteem. It's easier than you might think, and you'll be surprised by how quickly you start to *feel* better about yourself and your life.

SHOW AND TELL

There is a simple way you can raise your self-esteem—and lower your fear of rejection: *Think* self-loving thoughts and *act* in self-loving ways. Show and tell yourself how wonderful and worthwhile you are with thoughts and acts of self-kindness. Be your own loving parent and teacher by giving yourself the *unconditional love* you may never have received.

At this point, you may be asking,
"How do I do that?"

Keep reading; I'll show you how.

CHOOSE SELF-LOVING BELIEFS

"Belief consists in accepting the affirmations of the soul; unbelief, in denying them."
—Emerson

What are your beliefs about being gay?
Beliefs are assumptions. They are subjective truths

31

about yourself and your world. They are not *the* truth; they are merely *your* truth. Your feelings and behaviors mirror your beliefs. Your reality is the result of these assumptions.

It's no surprise that many gay women have problems with self-esteem; we live in a world that bombards us with messages about our "immorality" and "depravity" because we love someone of the same sex.

The only way you will ever have any peace of mind is to erase all this internalized propaganda of hate. Release yourself from the chains of conventional morality, and *decide* what you believe by listening to your own inner voice of guidance, your spiritual essence. *You* are the ultimate source of authority in your life; choose beliefs which help rather than harm your self-esteem.

SILENCE ALL SELF-CRITICISM

"Failure is, in a sense, the highway to success."
—Keats

Criticizing the self is more than just devastating to self-esteem. It's also an ineffective way to alter your behavior. You have been criticizing yourself for years, and you're still not who or where you want to be. Why? Because self-criticism makes you feel awful about yourself, and this depletes the energy and encouragement you need to effect lasting change.

Self-acceptance is essential to positive self-esteem. *Stop* putting yourself down, and *start* accepting yourself, including what you consider your undesirable traits. This doesn't mean you don't want to change or to grow. It also doesn't mean you're always content with yourself. It simply means you're not wasting time emotionally beating yourself up during your process of self-evolution.

The next time you make a mistake, rather than mercilessly berating yourself, try something new. Admit the mistake, *forgive yourself*, and let it go. This is a much more efficient way to modify behavior, because it helps you to focus your energy on finding solutions—what you can do "right"—rather than on dwelling on problems; i.e., what you did "wrong."

CLAIM YOUR PERSONAL POWER

Are you living your life your way?

If not, why?

Personal power is the ability to sculpt your own life by thinking, acting, and feeling as you *choose*. It's about living the life you want to live. "Power" is a provocative word. I don't mean power over others, as in manipulation or abuse. I am referring to power within the self. Claiming your personal power is an act that fortifies your sense of self.

And when you feel more in control of how you spend your time, you will be able to love yourself more.

Ask yourself:
"What do I want to do?"

Try to tune out all the voices that tell you what you should or what you shouldn't do; listen to the voice that tells you what would make *you* happy.

Pay attention to the answers this voice tells you. They reveal a path to a better self-esteem.

EXPAND YOUR COMFORT ZONE

Each of us has a different comfort zone, an emotional area beyond which we will not venture. Upon crossing this barrier, we feel afraid. This fear is imprisoning. Freedom lies in our ability to push past these self-imposed boundaries.

Before you can expand your comfort zone for meeting women, it's important to get a handle on how you really feel and those things that set off your panic button.

1. Take out a blank piece of paper and write "Meeting Women" at the top. Spend a few quiet moments thinking about this topic. What thoughts come up? Don't edit or critique your thoughts; just list them: *"I want ..." / "I wish ..." / "I fear ..." / "I feel ..." / "I should ..."* This process of taking a personal inventory will help you to identify your desires and fears.

2. Put your list aside. It's helpful for the thoughts to settle and for you to gain some perspective.

3. After a few days, take your list back out and look it over. On another sheet of paper, select one of the thoughts beginning with, "*I want ...*" or "*I wish ...*" and use it for the subject of a new page. For example, if you wrote, "*I want to have more lesbian friends,*" write "Lesbian Friends" at the top of your new page.

4. Every day, do one thing to move toward your goal. Write every step you take, big and small.

5. Make a new page for every one of your, "*I want ...*" and "*I wish ...*" thoughts. Repeat #4, above, for each page. With each step you take, you are expanding your comfort zone and improving your sense of self.

6. What if the specter of fear of rejection appears? Whenever it does, ask yourself: "*What will it cost me if I continue to allow this fear to control me?*"

7. If you have doubts about whether you can muster the stamina or courage to keep moving toward your goals, ask a friend to coach you. You can even be each other's coach. Make a deal with your friend that no fear-based excuse or rationale will be accepted. For example, when your fear of rejection is holding you back from calling a woman, have your friend keep telling you to, *"Call her anyway!"* until you do. Whatever excuse you come up with for not taking action, have your coach push you on.

8. All right, you've tackled the items on your list beginning with, *"I want ..."* and *"I wish ..."* Now, take a look at those thoughts beginning with, *"I should ..."* or *"I shouldn't ..."* These are negative messages you have learned from your parents, religious leaders, teachers, friends, and others.

   Take a good look at these comments, accept that they exist for the moment; then ignore them. They are nothing but toxic self-talk. (We'll go into this phenomenon more in the next chapter.)

The more you emotionally stretch yourself, the better you will feel about yourself. Be courageous; the rewards (a better self-image and social life) are worth the risks.

VISUALIZE

"The ancestor of every action is a thought."
—Emerson

Visualizations are daydreams; they are mental movies. When you visualize, you use your imagination to create pictures of how you would like things to be. Mentally rehearsing a positive outcome bolsters your belief that what you want is possible to have and it helps you feel good about yourself. This good feeling gives you the *self-confidence* you need to go out and do what you dream!

Learning to visualize is easy:

1. Picture in your mind's eye an ideal scene in which you meet a fantastic woman:
   Where are you?
   What are you doing?
   What do you look like?
   What is she doing?
   What does she look like?
   What are you saying to her?
   What is she saying to you?
   What are you thinking?
   What are you feeling?

2. Make this picture as vivid as possible by putting dynamic sounds, sights, and emotions into it. Visualize your desires with *excitement* and *passion*.

3. Here are some ideas, or invent your own:

You're at the commitment ceremony of your favorite lesbian couple. You notice a very cute woman by the buffet table. You observe her for a while, trying to figure out if she came with a date. She seems to be unescorted. You start moving in her direction. Just as you do, she turns around, sees you, and flashes you a big smile. You ...

You're at a lesbian fundraising event. In walks a woman who steals your breath away. You want to meet her, now. You watch her move about the hall talking and laughing with some friends. Finally, she leaves her friends and heads for the bar. Seizing the opportunity to get her alone, you head for the bar. You walk up to her, stand beside her, and ...

You're at the premiere of a new lesbian movie. While waiting in line, you spot an attractive woman looking your way.

She lowers her gaze as you look her way. The line starts moving into the theater. You reach her as she is about to look for a seat. You ask her …

You're at a party. You see a small group of women smiling and laughing; they look like they're having a lot of fun. Lately, you have been thinking you want to meet more gay women for friendship. Deciding you want to meet these women, you stand on the edge of the group, looking and listening for the right opportunity to join in. There is a lull in their banter: This is your chance. You walk up to the group, look at each woman, smile and …

You are the writer of your own mental movies. Draft perfect scripts; don't hold back on anything you might want.

REFRAME YOUR THOUGHTS

Most of us have been taught that self-worth is determined by what happens to us and how people react to us. This is a misguided belief system. Your experience of your life and yourself is based entirely upon your *perception*. Your feelings are not dictated by events in your outer world but by your inner world's *interpretation* of those events.

> *"There is nothing either good or bad, but thinking makes it so."*
> —Shakespeare

Thought reframing is a technique whereby you *shift* your perception of an event. When you alter your perception, you alter your experience. The classic example of thought reframing is seeing a glass as half-full rather than half-empty. Neither interpretation is right nor wrong, each is merely *your* interpretation.

Let's start with a simple interaction. Say you're in a situation where you see a woman and you approach her. Watching her reaction, you can tell she isn't interested in you. Does this mean you're a bad person? Someone not worth knowing?

In fact, it has no meaning except the meaning *you* give it; you decide what this experience means to you. The incident does not dictate your self-esteem; your *attitude* toward it does. You can choose to see it as validation of your unworthiness, and slink into the corner for the rest of the evening.

Or you can decide that this woman is not for you, you are still a woman of worth, and introduce yourself to another woman.

> *"My barn burned to the ground; now I can see the moon."*

This Japanese haiku beautifully captures the *power of perception* and the idea that each of us has a choice as to how to perceive something.

Your perception is your reality; *choose* to perceive events in self-affirming rather than self-denying ways.

Reframing failure

> *"They can because they think they can."*
> —Virgil

The word "failure" is filled with such negative connotations that many of us live our lives imprisoned by inaction purely out of fear of failing, of being seen as a failure. In the precarious arena of meeting other women, the risk of failure causes many of us to not approach each other. A woman may appear detached and indifferent when, in reality, she fears hearing the dreaded word, *"No."* Unfortunately, her behavior usually produces exactly what she most fears: alienation and rejection.

Choosing to label an experience as a failure can wreak havoc on your self-esteem. To overcome your fear of failure, you must shift your attitude toward failure. Reframe a situation which doesn't work out as you had planned as *feedback,* rather than failure. Label it a learning experience or an opportunity for growth. This will help you to look at your behaviors objectively and without self-criticism, and figure out what needs to be changed.

Once again, focusing on the solution rather than the problem is a far more productive way of achieving what you want. Demanding perfection every time you attempt to do something puts too much pressure on yourself; it is merely another way of punishing yourself. Give yourself a break, and your self-esteem a boost, by erasing the word failure from your vocabulary.

Reframing rejection

"It is the mind that maketh good of ill, that maketh wretch or happy, rich or poor.
—Spenser

Imagine you're at a dance club. You gather the courage to walk up to a woman and ask her to dance. She says, *"No."*

How do you feel about her response?

Although you may not like it, rather than choosing to feel bad because she turned you down, you can reframe the rejection by choosing to feel good because you overcame your fear and went up to her.

Because many of us believe our self-worth is rooted in other people's perception and treatment of us, we are shy about approaching women. Don't allow your sense of self to be tied up with whether or not someone wants to be your friend or lover. To allow other women to decide your self-esteem is to subject yourself to them in a most humiliating way. Why relinquish your self-esteem to anyone's negative opinion of you? Don't reject yourself because another woman rejects you.

You, and no one else, decides your sense of self. This is a profoundly important concept. It signals an end to the *"I need approval from others in order to approve of myself"* belief which may have been controlling your feelings and behaviors for too long. The job of determining your self-worth is back, finally, where it belongs—in your own mind.

How other women behave toward you is something you will never have any control over. What you do control is your *reactions* to other women's behaviors. Choose to feel and behave in self-supporting rather than self-defeating ways.

However, if you find yourself constantly rejected, this may be a signal that you're due for some self-examination. Reframe the rejection as an opportunity to learn more about yourself. Use the rejection as a stimulus for taking an honest look at your role in the rejection process. Because other women form their opinion of you based upon your opinion of yourself, they may reject you because you reject yourself. Your attitude, body language, facial expressions, and tone of voice broadcast your self-esteem.

If you're self-esteem is suffering, *don't* go to your next social engagement until you practice some tender self-talk.

SELF-TALK

"It is all within yourself, in your way of thinking."
—Aurelius

Inside each of us, a constant dialog, an incessant chatter is going on. Your conscious mind runs a continuous commentary as it sorts and processes billions of bits of information. Your thoughts are the mind's conclusions as to what this information means.

How you feel about yourself depends upon what you *say* to yourself. You can literally talk yourself into joy, misery, anger, or fear. This self-talk—things you say to yourself in the form of *thoughts*—dictates your feelings.

Toxic self-talk

Each of us is besieged by a self-hating inner voice. This voice, which is extremely critical, relentlessly tells us what is "wrong" with us.

It speaks to us about our "flaws," and it tells us over and over again how we are "not good enough": not pretty enough, talented enough, fit enough, smart enough, rich enough, thin enough, sexy enough—not anything enough.

This vicious voice is the result of our childhood (and adult) programming of unworthiness. It repeats every disapproving message we have ever

44

received. Our unconscious, unfortunately, remembers them all. Its strength, the hold it has on us, is in direct proportion to the amount of self-condemning messages we have been subjected to by parents, teachers, religious and cultural leaders and others. The louder your toxic self-talk, the lower your self-esteem.

This self-sabotaging voice produces feelings of fear, of ourselves and each other. The equivalent of verbal self-abuse, this toxic self-talk is poisonous to our self-esteem. We validate these toxic thoughts by feeling and behaving in self-defeating ways. In fact, with this vicious voice constantly reminding us of our "inadequacies," it is remarkable that any of us ever reach out to each other.

Listen to what other women say about themselves. Notice the self-deprecating remarks casually thrown into conversations. These negative comments cripple our sense of self. For many of us, the worst enemy we could ever have resides within us.

Our toxic self-talk is at full speed in social situations—

◆ As soon as a woman you meet says her name, your toxic self-talk begins: *"I am terrible at remembering names."*

As you are paying attention to this toxic thought rather than the woman's name, you haven't a clue as to what she just said.

45

◆ During a lull in a conversation, the vicious voice whispers:
"I never know what to say to a woman I've just met."

Sure enough, you don't know what to talk about, so you say nothing, and the conversation ends right there.

"I'm the only one here feeling uncomfortable."
"I'm no good at small talk."
"I look fat in these jeans."
"I feel awkward in social situations."
"My skin looks terrible today."
"I'm always shy around women I don't know."
"I hate my hair today."
"Why would she like me?"

For most of us, this running critique of how "imperfect" we are is unending; it's as though we have a tape in our head continuously playing the same self-hating songs. Self-sabotaging thoughts pop up with such speed and frequency we barely notice they are there. We have been living with this self-destructive voice for so long we don't even question the validity of its messages.

If you pay close attention to what you say to yourself, you will notice a disturbing number of self-invalidating remarks.

What are your "favorite" self-criticizing comments?

How often do you emotionally beat yourself up?

Try this exercise:

For a full day, list *all* of your self-defeating comments on paper. The purpose of this exercise is to make you more conscious of your toxic self-talk. The first step toward stopping it is becoming *aware* of it.

Tender self-talk

Thankfully, there is also a self-loving voice. This voice speaks in an affectionate and nurturing tone, and it reminds us of the supportive and self-empowering messages we have been exposed to (our unconscious, fortunately, also remembers them all).

This tender self-talk fills us with words of approval and appreciation. It is the magic key which opens the door of high self-esteem because when you *speak* lovingly to yourself, you *feel* good about yourself. Regardless of what happens in your outer world, you are always in control of your inner world through your self-talk.

The habit of tender self-talk requires solid commitment and faithful practice. If you don't practice tender self-talk everyday, your mind automatically goes back to spitting out toxic self-talk (unfair, but true).

Be persistent and patient with your process. Don't scold yourself (more toxic self-talk) if you notice self-demeaning thoughts. Be as gentle with yourself as you would be with a close friend. It took many years to develop a self-defeating pattern of thinking; it will take time and effort to develop a self-promoting one.

What will help you to accomplish your goal of transforming toxic self-talk into tender self-talk?

Manage your mind

Your thought patterns are nothing more than thought habits, and habits can be changed. You can manage your mind by consciously deciding on which thoughts to dwell.

Program your unconscious to erase the old toxic tapes and to play only tender tapes. *"STOP!"* is the first part of the plan you will use to turn off the toxic self-talk and turn on the tender self-talk.

Pay close attention to your self-talk. Whenever you notice the vicious voice chattering away, say, *"STOP!"* If necessary, say, *"STOP!"* several times; the point is to quiet the negative noise for a few blissful moments. Saying, *"STOP!"* tells your unconscious mind that self-hating thoughts are unacceptable and to stop sending them to the conscious mind.

After you clear your conscious mind of a toxic thought, START your tender self-talk. This teaches the unconscious mind to send only self-loving thoughts.

For example, when your vicious voice says, *"I look terrible tonight,"* say, *"STOP!"*

"*STOP!*" is the abbreviated version of:
  "*STOP! I refuse to think that garbage anymore.
  I release that toxic thought.*"

Then, immediately START your tender self-talk:
  "*I look and feel great tonight.*"
  "*I love myself.*"
  "*I am a woman of worth.*"

"*I am a woman of worth*" goes straight to the heart of the problem of fear of rejection. We fear meeting other women when we believe we aren't worth meeting.

Here's another example:
  You're at a party, and your attempt to make contact with a particular woman didn't work out as you had planned.

Your toxic self-talk consumes you:
  "*What a fool I made of myself!*"

Instead of letting this toxic thought sink in, say, "*STOP!*"

Then START your tender self-talk:
  "*It's all right that it didn't turn out the way I anticipated. I'm proud of myself for reaching out.*"

Repeating one of these statements will instantly make you feel more relaxed and confident. You will feel better about yourself when you practice the *"STOP!"* and START technique.

Use it; it works!

"What if ..."

Toxic self-talk can fuel our fear of rejection by consuming us with the question, *"What if ..."*

> *"What if she says, 'No'?"*
> *"What if I can't think of anything to talk about?"*
> *"What if she misinterprets my friendliness as a come-on?"*
> *"What if she ignores me?"*
> *"What if she isn't interested in dating me?"*
> *"What if she doesn't want to dance with me?"*
> *"What if she has a girlfriend?"*

Friends tell me that, sometimes, they want to introduce themselves to a woman but hesitate because they keep asking themselves *"What if ..."* questions. Preoccupation with *"What if ..."* leads to indecision and procrastination, and too many of us allow this nagging question to steal too many of our dreams. Don't allow *"What if ..."* to stop you from approaching other women.

"So what!" is the only reasonable answer to the unreasonable question *"What if ..."* I have never seen the floor open beneath the feet of a just-rejected woman and swallow her into an abyss (although sometimes we wish this would happen). If a woman you're interested in is not interested in you, it's not the end of the world; you'll be okay.

"STOP!" emotionally kicking yourself; START congratulating yourself for taking a chance. Good for you!

The next time a woman says, *"No"* to you ...

... use this rejection repair kit:

♦ Do not interpret her rejection of your invitation as a rejection of *you*. You have no idea why she may not want to speak or be with you. Her fear of rejection may have stolen her courage to be friendly. Whatever the reason, it's *her* problem, not yours.

♦ Say, *"STOP!"* to your blabbering toxic self-talk:
   "That was stupid to think she would go out with me."

START your comforting tender self-talk:
   "She just isn't for me, and that's okay. I

am still a woman of worth, and I am proud of myself for taking a risk."

◆ Let it go. Release the whole thing so you can be open to meeting more agreeable women.

◆ Remind yourself that the ability to withstand rejection is *crucial* for social success, and with every, *"No,"* you are one step closer to, *"Yes!"*

A personal anecdote

About two years ago, I was at a club in Ft. Lauderdale, Florida. I noticed a very attractive woman to whom I wanted to introduce myself. When I pointed out this woman to my friend, she gasped, *"I would never have the nerve to approach her; she's too beautiful."*

Refusing to let fear of rejection stop me from speaking to her, I took a deep breath, silently said, *"STOP!"* to the toxic self-talk swirling about my head, and began repeating:

"I love myself, and I love meeting women."

Feeling more relaxed and self-confident, I approached her, smiled, held out my hand, and said:

"Hi, I'm Rhona. Would you like to dance?"

As I stood there with my big smile and out-stretched arm, this woman looked at me, gave a forced smile, turned her back toward me and began speaking with another woman.

What was I going to do now??!!

I had to put into practice everything I preach. I refused to validate the toxic self-talk, which was now booming in my head:

> *"What a mistake it was to approach her. I made a complete idiot of myself! I should have known better than to ask such an attractive woman to dance!"*

As I walked back to my friend, who was watching all of this, I said, *"STOP!"* to my toxic self-talk (about twenty times), and I licked my wounds for a while by getting a drink of sparkling water and dancing with my friend.

Whenever the vicious voice would start telling me, again, what a jerk I had made of myself, I would say, *"STOP!"* and START practicing tender self-talk by congratulating myself for working on conquering my fear of rejection. I chose not to view the situation or, more importantly, myself as a failure. Instead, I chalked it up to *experience* and told myself this woman was obviously not for me.

Soon, I began to feel more comfortable with myself and the club. (I must admit I was happy to see the woman leave. Hey, I'm only human.)

Affirm yourself

Positive affirmations are forceful tools for training the mind to think only self-loving thoughts. Saying, *"I love myself"* and, *"I am a woman of worth,"* repeatedly and enthusiastically floods your unconscious with self-supporting messages. This strengthens your self-loving voice in hopes of, eventually, silencing your self-hating voice.

A positive affirmation is tender self-talk at its best as it is a strong reminder of self-worth. The more you practice this type of tender self-talk, the better you will feel about yourself. Toxic self-talk is merely a bad habit; positive affirmations teach your unconscious the good habit of tender self-talk.

Follow these easy steps to benefit from the self-esteem enhancing power of positive affirmations:

Design a simple self-loving statement. State it in the positive and in the present tense. When you affirm something, you are declaring that it is happening today, not in the future. Some examples are:

"I love myself, and I love meeting women."

"I am a woman of worth."

"I approve of and appreciate myself."

"I meet women confidently and easily."

"I am a great conversationalist."

"I deserve happy relationships."

Upon awakening in the morning and before retiring at night, spend five minutes saying your favorite affirmations. These are the best times to practice this type of tender self-talk because your unconscious mind is very receptive to suggestions right after you wake up and just before you go to sleep.

Write your affirmations on index cards or small pieces of paper, and affix them to places where you will consistently see them, such as a mirror, refrigerator, wallet, calendar, diary, or book.

Whenever your negative voice starts talking to you—and it will—talk back to it with one of your positive affirmations. This will silence it.

If possible, look in a mirror while declaring your self-affirming statements. Positive programming of the mind is reinforced if you have the visual cue of seeing yourself as well as the auditory cue of hearing yourself.

Experience each affirmation with full intensity, using every one of your senses. See it, hear it, and feel it. This kind of attention helps your unconscious to absorb the affirmations more quickly.

Create a one-word mantra out of an affirmation. For example, if your affirmation is,
"I am a woman of worth," you could use the
word, *"worth"* as your mantra. Repeat it to
yourself whenever you feel your self-assur-
ance waning. This will help you to feel
more confident.

Does it feel strange to say these affirmations? It
might. At first, you may even resist saying them. You
have been saying nasty things to yourself for years;
saying nice things may feel unfamiliar and uncomfortable. Keep at it! It takes commitment and perse-
verance to integrate these self-loving messages into
your psyche. Conscientiously repeat your affirmations everyday, and you *will* notice a dramatic differ-
ence in the way you feel.

DAILY SELF-CARE: ACTS OF SELF-LOVE

> *"To affect the quality of the day,*
> *that is the highest of arts."*
> —Thoreau

Daily self-care is the next leap forward on the path
toward high self-esteem. When you *act* in self-loving
ways, you communicate to your unconscious that
you believe you are a woman of worth. This *belief*
leads to feeling good about yourself.

Everyday, ask yourself:
"What can I do today to take good care of myself?"

Then do it!
Here are some suggestions:

◆ Call a friend you haven't spoken to in a long time. You both will feel happy you did.

◆ Laugh.
Watch a funny movie or TV show; read a humorous book; swap jokes with a friend. Laughter is strong medicine; you can't help but feel good when you laugh.

◆ Take a nap.
After a hard day, a nap is sometimes exactly what you need to recharge your emotional and physical batteries.

◆ Surround yourself with supportive people.
Surrounding yourself with supportive people is indispensable to the continuing process of improving your self-esteem. Remove people from your life who criticize and belittle you. They only serve to

hinder you on your trek toward a better sense of self.

◆ Support yourself.

Every woman struggles with feelings of low self-esteem, to one degree or another. Support groups offer a comforting place to share your feelings with other women. Check local papers for women's support groups.

◆ Give yourself a half hour each day to do *whatever* you like.

◆ Appreciate Yourself.

You will feel more self-loving when you take the time to notice and appreciate your unique and wonderful qualities.

Take out a pen and paper, and write the answers to the following questions:

"What are my favorite physical characteristics?
Look in the mirror and pick out your favored features. Your eyes, hair, stomach, arms, hands, feet, legs ...

"What are my favorite emotional and intellectual characteristics?"
For example: You're an excellent listener;

you have a good sense of humor; you're loyal; you have a quick wit.

"What do I believe I do well?"
Play softball, play golf, write short stories, sing, dance, cook ...

Focus on what you *do* like about yourself. Applauding all the terrific parts of you will make you feel great!

◆ Get Moving.
Being physically active is a great way to show how much you value yourself. And its fun, too! Jog, rollerblade, play tennis, walk, dance, do aerobics, lift weights, play racquetball, play softball, swim, bike, ski ...

◆ Volunteer.
When you give *of* yourself, you give *to* yourself. Pick up your local lesbian and gay paper, and find an organization or two which could use your help. You'll both benefit from it!

◆ Eat Healthy Foods.
Love your body by feeding it nutritious foods. Your body (and your mind) will love you back.

◆ Take a warm bath with aromatherapy oils or salts.

◆ Do nothing.
Take the phone off the hook. Put on some soothing music. Stretch out on the couch. Take a deep breath, and relax. You deserve it!

◆ Praise Yourself.
Every day, give yourself at least one compliment. It can be for anything: your hair, your work, your healthy eating habits, your one hour work out, your assertiveness in approaching women, etc. The purpose of this exercise is to get you into the habit of honoring yourself. Start today. You'll feel great for it!

◆ Read a book you have been wanting to read.

◆ Meditate.
Meditation enables you to deeply relax. With practice, you will experience a remarkable serenity. If you want to find out more about meditation, there are innumerable books on the topic. Also, classes and workshops on meditation are given throughout the country. Check out a local community calendar for information.

◆ If you enjoy cooking, take the time to cook a terrific meal for yourself.

◆ Write your feelings in a journal.

Writing is very therapeutic. Having a safe place to express your feelings is a terrific way to work through life's challenges. It doesn't matter if you think you can't write well (say, *"STOP!"* to this toxic self-talk). Do it anyway. You're writing for your eyes only.

Don't worry if at times you feel like criticizing yourself for not being further along on the road toward self-esteem. Chronicling your thoughts, feelings, and experiences allows you to observe your progress. This helps to quiet self-criticism as it reminds you of how far you have come. Change is a process; be patient with yourself.

◆ Express Yourself Creatively.

Do you like writing, sculpting, painting, singing, dancing, playing a musical instrument, cooking, etc.? Choose your own outlet for creative expression, and enjoy!

◆ Get a massage.

◆ Get your favorite flowers for your home.

◆ Take a yoga class.

◆ Get help.

Discussing deeply personal issues of self-worth with a good therapist can be wonderfully self-healing. There are many *invaluable* emotional benefits to be gained from exploring the origins of a damaged self-esteem in a safe and encouraging environment.

◆ Find your spiritual connection.

Feeling aligned with a spiritual force helps you on your journey of self-love as it imbues you with a sense of *inner peace*.

◆ Be patient.

Be wary of the pitfall of impatience. When you are impatient with yourself, you put yourself in the wrong; it is a form of self-punishment. The tools I have recommended are very effective, but they are not an instant cure to the disease of low self-esteem. Be *gentle* with yourself through your process of self-discovery.

"Adopt the pace of nature; her secret is patience."

—Emerson

MOVE FORWARD

You are faithfully practicing your self-esteem building tools. You are *thinking* and *behaving* in more self-loving ways, and your self-concept, how you *feel* about yourself, is steadily improving. You're ready for "Part Two: The Outer World."

Part Two

The Outer World

"Nothing external to you has any power over you."
—Emerson

Chapter Three

Meeting Compatible Women

"Luck occurs at the crossroads of preparation and opportunity."
—Anonymous

"When I first came out, I didn't have any les-bian friends. I was living in a small town, and I didn't have a clue as to how to find other gay women. I discovered a local women's bookstore, and I looked on the community bulletin board. I saw a couple of announcements for softball teams. Even though I wasn't a softball player, I thought I could meet women if I joined a team. I didn't like the softball ... or the women. It was a lonely time for me."

"I live in a large city. There are two lesbian bars and one lesbian social group. I don't go to the bars because I've been sober for two years, and I don't like being around alcohol or drinkers. I have some lesbian friends, but I would like to ex-pand my social circle. There is no group dedicat-ed to what I really love to do—bicycling. I won-der how I could start a lesbian bicycling club."

"When I was single, I used to go to a lot of bars and parties. It was easy for me to meet other sin-gle women. I've been in a committed relation-ship for four years. My lover and I would like to meet other couples with whom to have dinner, watch movies, go to concerts, go on vacations, etc. It's been hard for us to meet other lesbian couples; they don't seem to go out much."

"Having a life partner is very important to me, but I can't seem to find her. I can't stand going

to the bars. It's impossible to meet anyone there. Everyone seems so uptight and unfriendly. I don't know, maybe I'm the one who is uptight. The whole lesbian social scene is frustrating and depressing. I've given up; I don't think I'll ever find a woman to share my life with."

"My thirteen year relationship broke up six months ago. When I looked for emotional support, I realized I didn't have any close lesbian friends. I guess I poured all of my emotional energy into my relationship with my lover. I now realize what a mistake that was. So, here I am at fifty-two, single, and looking for friends. Forget the bars. Everyone is so much younger than me. I feel like a grandmother in those places. Finding women my own age is hard. I know they're out there; I just don't know where."

Many gay women express dissatisfaction with the lesbian social scene. Over and over again I hear women talk about how hard it is to meet the women they want to meet.

Here are some basic principles on how to meet compatible women.

DO WHAT YOU LOVE TO DO

The easiest way to meet the women you want to meet is to do what you love to do. Almost any enjoyable activity can be a bridge to meeting compatible women. Love to cook? Share your enthusiasm by joining (or starting) a cooking group. Enjoy reading? Get involved in a book discussion group. It's easy to indulge your passions, and to meet like-minded women! All it takes is some *self-awareness* as to your interests, and *commitment* to sharing those interests with others.

When you do what you *want* to do, rather than what you think you should do, you make meeting women *fun* instead of forced. You're also so busy enjoying yourself you forget to feel insecure and self-conscious.

WHAT DO YOU LOVE TO DO?

Make your own "What I Love to Do" list. Here are some ideas:

Rollerblading	Two-stepping
Playing racquetball	Playing cards
Scuba diving	Camping
Skiing	Fine dining
Bowling	Sailing
Going to the theater	Bicycling
Going to concerts	Playing golf
Horseback riding	Reading
Seeing movies	Writing
Cooking	Water skiing
Hiking	Fishing

Ice skating	Walking
Going to the beach	Playing volleyball
Surfing the internet	Playing board games
Acting	White water rafting
Dancing	Going to museums
Playing softball	Painting
Running	Sculpting
Fast walking	Skydiving
Lifting weights	Traveling
Swimming	Playing tennis
Wind surfing	Sightseeing

Pick one, two, or ten of these activities if you want.

"WHO DO I WANT TO MEET AND WHY DO I WANT TO MEET HER?"

Most of us have little idea about what qualities we are looking for in a woman and what role we want her to play in our life.

To figure out *who* you want to meet, be specific about those *qualities* which are important to you. Someone who is outgoing? Funny? Independent? Quiet? Athletic? Financially secure? Sincere? Sexy?

To figure out *why* you want to meet someone, be specific about what *role* you want a woman to play in your life. Are you looking for a lover? A life part-ner? A bicycling buddy? A confidante? A bar and club chum? A traveling companion? A close friend? An occasional sex partner?

Answering these questions will help you to meet the right women. The "right women" for you are women with whom you effortlessly develop a rapport. You are most likely to form a rapport (an emotional bond) with women who share your interests, values, beliefs, and lifestyle. We feel comfortable being around like-minded women because compatibility creates connection. Think about your closest friends. They may not be exactly like you, but they probably share many of your interests and values.

DESIGN A SOCIAL PLAN

If you were contemplating starting your own business, you would create a business plan, right? Well, planning a social life is at least as important as planning a business life. So, why not design a social plan? A social plan is a plan of *action*. It identifies who you want to meet and why you want to meet her.

To design your own social plan, ask yourself:

"What qualities am I looking for in a friend?"
(Who you want to meet)

"What qualities am I looking for in a lover?"
(Who you want to meet)

"What are my present relationship goals?"
(Why you want to meet her)

"What are my future relationship goals?"
(Why you want to meet her)

For example, you may answer:

"The qualities I am looking for in a friend: independence; enthusiasm; sincerity; optimism; and loyalty."

"The qualities I am looking for in a lover: the same qualities I want in a friend; and passion."

"My present relationship goals: being in a fun romantic relationship; and having friends who like to play golf, go to the theater, and dance."

"My future relationship goals: having a life partner with whom to have a child; being around other lesbian couples with children; and retiring with my partner to Florida."

Too many of us passively wait for the right women, hoping they will magically cross our path. Looking for compatible women without having a social plan is like driving to a foreign destination without a map. Knowing where you are going helps you to plan the best way of getting there.

Chapter Four

Where the Women Are

*"My strength lies solely
in my tenacity."*
—Pasteur

"A few years ago, I was single and searching for a lover. I was unhappy with the bar scene, so I decided to give the personals a try by responding to several ads. It didn't work out too well for me. I wasted a lot of money and time because I didn't find a relationship. I met a few nice women, but I wasn't interested in dating them. I don't think I would do it again."

"When I moved to a new city, I didn't know any gay women. I was reading a local lesbian newspaper and noticed the personals section. I put in an ad in hope of finding friends, and, possibly, a lover. I was happily surprised when seventeen women responded to my ad. I didn't find a lover, but I did find some great friends. The ad jumpstarted my social life. Four years later, I'm still close with some of the women I met. I would recommend it as a good way of meeting women."

GET PERSONAL

Most lesbian and gay publications have a personals section which many women read and use. A personal ad can be a *great* way to meet the women you want to meet!

But—be warned: Women who place or answer an ad believing the personals is the route to finding Ms. Right risk having their hopes dashed. Demanding that a personal ad lead you to a life partner may leave you feeling very disappointed.

A personal ad works best for a woman who sees it as *a* tool for building her social life rather than *the* tool for finding "the one." You will enjoy the personals process much more if you don't let your desire to find a lover blind you to being open to making new friends.

Before jumping into the personals pool, ask yourself:

▼ *"Will I be satisfied if I don't meet 'the one'?"*
▼ *"Am I willing to expend the necessary time, energy, and money to meet women this way?"*
▼ *"Will this be a fun way for me to meet women?"*

If the answer to any of these questions is, *"No,"* you may want to consider other options for meeting women.

Ask your friends who have participated in the personals about their experiences.

▼ *"What made you decide to place or answer a personal ad?"*
▼ *"What were your goals?"*
▼ *"Were you satisfied with the results?"*
▼ *"Did you meet a friend or lover?"*
▼ *"Do you have any advice on writing or answering an ad?"*
▼ *"How many ads have you placed?"*

▼ *"How many ads have you answered?"*
▼ *"Would you use the personals again?"*

Their impressions may assist you in deciding whether or not the personals is a good tool for you.

Writing the ideal personal ad

The ideal personal ad is an honest, upbeat, distilled version of who you are, who you want to meet, and why you want to meet her.

1. Tell the truth.
   It's trite but true: Honesty is the best policy. Lying (or exaggerating the truth) about yourself is a lousy way to begin any kind of relationship. Be honest about your age, weight, relationship status (unattached or involved), sexual orientation (bisexual or lesbian), disability, or anything else which may unfairly surprise someone. Show who you are, and allow a woman to decide if she wants to meet you.

2. Be positive.
   We've all read many ads that contain sentiments like these:

"I'm embarrassed that I'm resorting to this."

"I wonder if I'm the only sane lesbian left."

"I hate being single."

"I can't believe I'm doing this."

"I swore I would never do this."

"I'm disgusted with the lesbian social scene."

"If I don't find a decent woman soon, I'm going back to men."

Don't write an ad when you are feeling despondent. The universal law of attraction states we attract to us what we are. If your ad has a bitter, angry tone to it, you wil attract bitter, angry women. Unless you're looking for this type of woman, work on lifting your spirits *before* you work on writing your ad. Let your happy and healthy self shine through by keeping your ad positive.

3. Be specific.

Many ads are vague, relying on such trite words as "attractive" to convey meaning. "Attractive" is such an overused adjective that it has been gutted of all meaning. If you want to tell women you are attractive, recite your vital statistics (brown curly hair, 5'3", 112 lbs.), and let your readers reach their own conclusions.

You want to encourage responses from the women you want to meet and to discourage responses from the women you don't. Make your ad do most of the work for you. The more specific you are about who you are, who you want to meet, and why you want to meet her, the less time you will spend sifting through letters from incompatible women.

4. Describe who you are.

Describe your quintessential qualities by completing the statement, *"I am ..."*

funny	independent
patient	Christian
spontaneous	loyal
quiet	feminine
discreet	passionate
creative	optimistic
butch	gentle
respectful	big
Jewish	monogamous
"out"	transsexual
adventurous	petite
extroverted	non-monogamous
African American	vegan
college educated	gay
financially secure	tall

romantic   honest
athletic   compassionate
bisexual   reliable ...

Describe your main interests by listing several entries from your "What I Love to Do" list.

5. Describe who you want to meet and why you want to meet her. For instance:

A monogamous gay woman for a serious romantic relationship

A life partner with whom to have a child

A discreet gay woman for a passionate affair

African American lesbians for friendship

A handsome butch for a romantic relationship

Sincere and loyal friends

Women who like to hike

A sweet and gentle lover who is over forty

A financially secure lover who likes cats and wants to live in the country

Single women looking to form a social group

Sober women who enjoy going to sober dances

Jewish lesbians with whom to attend services at the lesbian and gay temple

Vegetarians interested in forming a veg-
etarian pot-luck dinner group

Lesbians who love to wind surf

Another married bisexual woman for a
clandestine affair

A woman of transgendered experience
looking for a committed relationship

Other happy and committed lesbian couples for friendship

A golfing buddy...

6. Other helpful ideas on writing a great
ad:

Look at the personal ad section of your
local lesbian and gay paper or magazine.
Which ads appeal to you? To which ads
would you respond? If an ad interests
you, ask yourself what you like about it
and try to capture its essence in your
own ad.

Let friends critique your copy. They can
be a great resource for constructive criticism and worthwhile suggestions. If you
are having trouble writing an ad you
like, put it aside for a few days. The time

away from it may be what you need to get your thoughts on paper.

Describe who you are, who you want to meet, and why you want to meet her in fifty words or less.

Don't make writing the ad a painstaking project; *have fun* with it.

Answering your responses

1. Choosing which responses to answer:

   Approach each response with an open mind and an open heart. Look past the nervous voice or self-conscious language to see if there is a sincere and caring energy.

   Discard angry responses. You gain nothing by consciously inviting negative women into your life.

   Be wary of desperation. Listen to the intensity of a response. Does your respondent seem desperate to meet you? If so, you might not want to respond to her. You want to bring women into your life who want you to befriend them, not to save them.

2. Responding. When you finish wading through your responses, it's time to start calling some of the women behind them. There are some simple rules to keep in mind:

If you get an answering machine, don't refer to your personal ad. Someone else might hear the message, and embarrassing a woman is not the best way to begin a relationship with her. Simply state your first name, home phone number, and the best time to reach you.

If she is home when you call, tell her who you are and remind her of the ad you wrote. Because she may have answered other ads, you want to make her comfortable by helping her to identify your ad.

Engage her in light conversation. Describe why you enjoyed her response and why you decided to call her. Don't make your first phone contact an interrogation. It's best to leave questions like, *"Have you ever been in therapy?"* and,

"What was your role in the break-up of your last relationship?" for another time.

Don't stay on the phone for three hours. It isn't necessary to find out *everything* about her during the first call. Be careful of the lesbian tendency to leap toward instant intimacy. There is a very old, (and, unfortunately, very true) lesbian joke:

Question: What do lesbians do on their second date?
Answer: Move in together

Don't rush things. Let intimacy unfold gradually. Focus on having fun, and see what develops.

If you feel comfortable with her, arrange to get together with her. Make it a quick meeting in a public place. It's a mistake to commit to spending an entire day with a woman you have only met over the phone. You can't determine if you've made a friendship or love connection until you meet face-to-face. There is something about in-person chemistry that can't be predicted by phone conversations, regardless of how many you have.

If you two hit it off, great! You can agree to get together at another time. If you don't, you can make a smooth and gracious exit.

Inform her you will be carrying or wearing something so she can effortlessly identify you: a blue knapsack, a tan book, a black baseball cap, a white rose, whatever.

End the phone call on an up-note: *"It's been great speaking with you; I'm looking forward to meeting you."*

Answering an ad

Good responses to personal ads contain the same vital elements of good ads—heart, soul, and clarity. Always tell the truth about who you are, who you want to meet, and why you want to meet her. Describe why her ad interested you, and why you decided to respond to it. Be generous in your appraisal of her ad, as a genuine compliment builds a rapport. (We'll go into more on this in Chapter Six, "Talking.")

If responding by letter, be brief. The writer may have received thirty other responses, so don't write your life story. If you're answering via a 900 number, you have an even greater incentive to be brief—

money. Many phone response lines charge $1.95 per minute, which can quickly add up.

Let your reply showcase how emotionally healthy and positive you are. Don't use it as an opportunity to vent your disappointment with the lesbian community. Save your frustration for your friends or your therapist, not a woman you would like to call you.

If responding via letter:

◆ Don't send a generic photocopy or computer-generated letter; it's tacky. A handwritten letter or card is much more impressive. It lets a woman know that you consider her ad special enough to take the time to hand write a response.

◆ If you also placed an ad, don't send it as your response; again, it's tacky. Show her what a sensitive and caring woman you are by sending an answer specifically tailored to her ad.

◆ Write your reply as neatly as possible.

◆ Check it for spelling and grammatical errors.

◆ Don't worry about selling yourself to her. Just be your best self: your loving self. That's more than enough.

Protect yourself

Be smart. Guard against unwelcome attention and unpleasant situations by following a few fundamental rules:

Don't list your name or phone number in your personal ad.

Exercise caution when speaking to your respondent for the first time. Feel her out before you reveal information about where you live and where you work. After you feel at ease with her give her *only* your home phone number.

Protect your anonymity when answering an ad by mail. Don't reveal your work phone number or address, your last name, or your home address. Only include your home phone number so she can contact you. You must protect yourself. You have no idea who placed the ad; it could be a leech, a psychopath, or even a man!

Always arrange your first date in a public place. Going to her home or having her come to yours is not a good idea.

Choose a positive perception

How you perceive your personal ad experience is *your* choice:

Negative: *"I will have wasted my time and money if I don't find 'the one.'"*

Positive: *"Whatever happens, I am proud of myself for reaching out to other women."*

Choose to see the personals as an exciting adventure. Keep it light, have fun, don't make finding a lover a requirement for success, and be open to new experiences. You never know who you may meet ...

USE A DATING SERVICE

"About a year ago, I joined a dating service for gay women. I thought it might be a fun way to meet other single women. I was mistaken. There were only thirty-four women registered with this service. Most of them were too old for me. I went on four dates in two months, all of which were duds. I will never join another dating service."

"When I moved to a state where I knew only a few other lesbians, I joined a lesbian dating service. Because a friend of mine had met her lover through this particular service, I decided to give

it a go. I met eight women in two months. All of them were very nice. I didn't find a lover, but I made several new friends. It was a good experience for me."

Women who have had experiences with lesbian dating services are like everyone else: Some have a good time; some do not. As with everything, perception is paramount. A woman who joins a service expecting to meet the love of her life will probably be the most dissatisfied. The one who views it as merely another way to meet women will probably be the most satisfied.

To decide if a dating service may be a good way for you to meet women, ask yourself:

▼ *"Will I be satisfied if I don't meet 'the one'?"*
▼ *"Am I willing to expend the time, energy, and money necessary to meet women this way?"*
▼ *"Will this be a fun way for me to meet women?"*

If you decide to go this route, before choosing a specific service, ask the service:

▼ *"How many women are presently registered with your service?"*
▼ *"What is the average age of the women?"*
▼ *"Where do most of these women live?"*
▼ *"What are your fees?"*

▼ *"What services are included in these fees?"*
▼ *"Do you offer a money back guarantee if I am dissatisfied with your service?"*
▼ *"How long have you been in business?"*
▼ *"May I call some satisfied customers to ask them about your service?"*

Call the references, and ask them:

▼ *"When were you a member of the dating service?"*
▼ *"Did the service introduce you to women you wanted to meet?"*
▼ *"Were you satisfied with the service?"*
▼ *"Was the service worth what you paid?"*
▼ *"Are you aware of women who were dissatisfied with the service?"*
▼ *"Would you recommend the service to a friend?"*

Using a dating service can be worth your investment of time, energy, and money if you approach it with the right attitude: View it as *a* way, rather than *the* way, to meet women, and be emotionally available for a lover or a friend.

GET OUT

If you live in a metropolitan area, you may be fortunate enough to have a lesbian and gay community center near you. If you do, check it out. It can be a veritable gold mine of opportunities for meeting women. Call or write the center to get a schedule of groups and events. If you decide to start your own group—what a great idea!—the center may be a perfect place to hold your meetings.

GET INVOLVED

Find your town's lesbian and gay organizations. Volunteering your time to a worthy lesbian and gay cause is a wonderful way to serve your community and to discover women with a similar interest.

GO TO A PRIDE PARADE

If your city hosts an annual lesbian and gay pride parade, go! It's the best party of the year. When I attended my first pride parade in New York City, I was overwhelmed (and overjoyed) by the hundreds of thousands of gay women and men marching and watching. Participating in a pride march is extraordinarily self-empowering. It's also an unrivaled opportunity to meet other lesbians.

STOP BY THE BARS ... AND READ

Find your neighborhood lesbian bars and clubs. If

you don't like the bar scene, go in, pick up the lesbian literature, and leave. Many newsletters, newspapers, and magazines announcing local lesbian groups and activities are available for free in such places. These publications are terrific resources for finding other women. Most contain a directory of professional, social, support, religious, athletic, and political groups as well as a schedule of events, such as, readings, dances, movies, concerts, softball games, parties, and political rallies.

And, with your new sense of self-confidence, you might decide to stay a while and try out your spectacular social skills.

PICK UP A BOOK—AND MAYBE A WOMAN

Frequent the lesbian and gay bookstores in your area. In smaller towns, these bookstores can serve as informal lesbian and gay community centers. Usually they have bulletin boards as well as lesbian publications listing various groups and activities in your town.

You may even find an adorable book lover in the last aisle.

TALK TO YOUR FRIENDS

"I'm out to my mom. One day, I casually mentioned I wanted to meet more gay women for

friendship. I was shocked when, two weeks later, she gave me the phone number of a gay woman she met at work. I called the woman; we got together the next night. That was two years ago, and we're still friends. I never thought my mother would help me find women!"

Talk to your friends about their friends. There may be women in their social network who could become a part of your social network, and vice versa. Social networking is as important to your personal life as business networking is to your professional life. Networking is about building relationships. It involves sharing resources, ideas, and information with others. Give generously of your time, energy, and support, and others will return the favor.

Share your "What I Love to Do" list and your social plan with everyone in your life with whom you feel comfortable. Enlist your friends' help in expanding your social circle. They can be terrific scouts. Most likely, your friends will be happy to be on the look-out for compatible women for you to meet.

DO IT YOURSELF

"I love reading books. I want to meet other literary lesbians. There are two lesbian social groups in my area, but they both revolve around sports. If there was a lesbian book discussion group, I would definitely join."

"We bought a house here about eight months ago. Meeting other lesbian couples in the area to socialize with is important to us. There is a singles social group, but no couples social group. We were wondering about how to start one."

"Bicycling is my passion. I love taking short and long trips. Finding other women who share this passion would be fantastic. There is a women's softball league, but no bicycling club."

If you can't find a group which sponsors an activity you love, start a group yourself!

It's easy. All it takes is the *decision* to do it, and the *commitment* to follow through with your decision. If you are willing to spend a little time, effort, and money, you can easily create the social life of your dreams!

Starting a group in three simple steps

Let's say you wanted to start a lesbian bicycling group.

How would you do it?

1. Choose a name. In four words or less, give as much information about your club as possible. For example, after discussing possible names with some of your friends, you settle on "Gay Women's Bicycling Club."

2. Broadcast the news.

Tell all of your friends about the new club. Even if your friends aren't cycling enthusiasts, they may know a woman who is.

Stop by your favorite lesbian and gay print shop (it's nice to support our own), and print up flyers announcing your group. Describe the purpose of the group, and some of its activities. Leave blank spaces to write in the date, time, and location of the next event. Remember to always guard your safety: Only pick a busy time and safe public place in which to meet.

> ### Gay Women's Bicycling Club
>
> Do you love bicycling?
>
> Do you want to meet other bicycling-loving lesbians?
>
> Our fun-loving group meets the first and third Saturday of every month at various parks around the city. We also take short and long bike trips.
>
> Join at the _____ entrance of _____ Park, on Saturday, _____ at _____.
>
> We look forward to meeting YOU!

Stop by your local lesbian bars, clubs, and bookstores and ask the owner or manager if you can leave some flyers. Most places will be happy to help you spread the word.

While at these bars, clubs, and bookstores, pick up the local lesbian newsletters, newspapers, and magazines. If the publication has a community calendar section, it will usually list the event free of charge. Call the publication several weeks before the scheduled event with information as to where and when.

> **Gay Women's Bicycling Club**
> Join our fun-loving group at the
> _____ entrance of
> _____ Park on Saturday,
> _____ at ____ .
> **We look forward to meeting YOU!**

If you live near a lesbian and gay community center, call to inquire about dropping off flyers. Also, ask to be included in the calendar of events.

If there is a local television or radio lesbian and gay program, call the station to query about a community calendar. If the program has one, provide the necessary information.

3. Have fun!

Using the personals to start a group

Placing a personal ad might be the ideal group starting tool for you if you want to get to know women one-on-one before meeting them in a group setting. Also, an ad is a good way to screen women, and it can be more convenient than distributing flyers and placing announcements.

For example, you and your lover want to start a lesbian couples social group.

> Join our new Lesbian Couples Social Group. Meet other lesbian couples while enjoying fun social activities—movies, parties, pot-luck dinners, day trips, etc. We look forward to meeting YOU!

Decide on the date and location of your first activity. Make it at least a month away to give everyone time to plan. Hopefully, a majority of your respondents will be able to attend.

As always, exercise caution when speaking to these women for the first time. And, again, schedule the activity in a public place at a busy time.

SURF THE NET

"I was bored one night and I decided to search for lesbians on the internet. I met a woman in a lesbian chat room. We actually had cyber sex! She lived in my city, so we made a date for the next night. The date was okay, but there was no chemistry. There was so much sexual energy between us on-line and so little in person. I never spoke to her again, on- or off-line."

"I met a lover from an on-line lesbian bulletin board. We were living in different states, so setting up a time and place to meet was a challenge. We communicated by computer, phone, and letter for two months before we actually met. We had a long distance relationship for over two years. I have met several other women this way; I think the bulletin boards are a good way to find other lesbians."

"I met a man on the internet. He pretended to be a lesbian; he was very convincing. I began to get suspicious when he had excuse after excuse as to why he couldn't meet me in person. Other friends have told me similar stories. I don't like the lesbian chat rooms and bulletin boards. There are too many straight men masquerading as gay women."

Women's experiences meeting other women on the net run from very positive to very negative. If you view the internet as merely *another* means of finding women, it could be a lot of fun.

The biggest problem with meeting on-line is that you have absolutely no idea about someone's true identity. Always *protect* your anonymity. Never give anyone your last name, work or home phone number, or work or home address when you first meet. After you feel comfortable with your new cyberpal, offer *only* your home phone number. If she (or he) does turn out to be emotionally unstable, you can always have it changed.

If you decide to meet in person, do so only in a public place at a busy time. Don't go to her home; don't invite her to yours.

Chapter Five

Making Contact

"Action is eloquence."
—Shakespeare

"I was invited to a party. I went thinking it would be a great place to meet women, but I had a horrible time. When I walked in, there were a lot of women, but I didn't know anyone besides the hostess. I felt intimidated and uneasy the whole night. I couldn't relax and get into the swing of the party. I stood by myself most of the time. It was a disappointing night."

Chapters Three and Four, "Meeting Compatible Women" and "Where the Women Are" showed you *what to do* and *where to go* to find the women you want to meet. In this chapter, I will discuss *how to make contact* with them.

WARMING UP

To play any game well, you must first warm up and exercise your muscles. Just as a smart softball player needs to stretch her physical muscles before a game, a master mingler must stretch her social muscles before meeting women.

It is unreasonable to expect yourself to be at ease as soon as you walk into a social gathering. Whenever you place yourself in a new situation, you need time to adjust emotionally to your new surroundings.

Take a tour

The easiest way to regain your emotional balance is to take a tour of your new environment. For a few minutes, walk around and pay attention to what is going on. Don't judge; merely observe.

Notice the women, of course, but also the action.

Where is the bar?

Where is the food?

Where is the bathroom?

Where is the hostess?

Where is the disc jockey?

Where is the dance floor?

Who do I know?

Who is standing alone?

Who appears shy?

How many groups of women are there?

How many women are coupled, either as friends or lovers?

What are the activities?

The simple act of taking a tour and observing the scene helps to warm up those social muscles because you're changing an unfamiliar space into a familiar one. This makes you feel more at home.

Take a second tour. This time start to process what you're observing. If you're nervous, be careful not to make hasty judgments about what you see. Because we all have a natural tendency to project our own feelings of discomfort onto an environment, your perceptions could be distorted by your anxiety.

During this second tour, ask yourself:

"Do I want to be here?"

"Will I have fun here?"

"Can I meet compatible women here?"

If you, unhesitatingly, answer, *"No,"* to all three questions, you may want to leave. But, before leaving, ask yourself one more question:

"Am I leaving out of fear of meeting new women?"

If there is any chance that the answer to this question might be, *"Yes,"* don't leave. Give yourself more time to warm up.

Now, take a third tour. This time, become curious about who is there and what is going on. As you move through the crowd, make eye contact, smile, and say, *"Hi!"* Being friendly *now* makes it easier to approach women *later*.

Usually, we are so preoccupied with what other women think about us, we forget to notice who and what is around us. When you concentrate on what's happening "out there," you are less aware of your toxic self-talk:

"I always feel nervous meeting new women. I never know what to say ..."

When you tune out the toxic tapes and tune in to your environment, you will feel less apprehensive.

Remind yourself that you're not the only one feeling anxious. Most of the other women in the room also feel that way. Except, of course, for those women who have already read this book!

Offer your help

> *"I joined a lesbian social group to meet women. I went to a couple of dances, but I was too shy to talk to anyone. A friend suggested I join the dance committee. So, at the next dance, I was at the front door, taking tickets. I met a lot of women there. After my shift was over, I talked to some of them. I had a lot of fun. Since that night, I work the door at every dance."*

A good way to meet other women in a group is to offer your help. Adopting an active role in an organization increases your visibility, thereby giving other women the chance to notice you and to make contact with you. Recall a basic tenet of life: The more you *give*, the more you *get*.

Also, offering to help gives you something to do besides feeling self-conscious. If you have a built-in reason for making contact, you won't feel as tense. Whatever you do, use it as an opportunity to meet and greet.

Do offer your help for a while; don't offer it all day

or night. If you work the entire event, you lose your chance for continued contact with the women you briefly met while working.

Participate

Participating in an activity is a much more effective way to warm up your social muscles than being a spectator. Participation distracts you from your toxic self-talk, it gets you noticed, and it's fun. It's also a relaxing way to meet women as the activity lends the reason for making contact.

YOUR FIRST STEPS

Enter with confidence

The very act of entering a roomful of strangers causes anxiety in most of us. In Chapter Two, "Self-Esteem," I discussed *"STOP!"* and START. This *"STOP!"* and START exercise will help you to enter with confidence.

Your toxic self-talk might say:

"People will stop what they're doing and stare at me."

This toxic thought causes you to walk in feeling nervous and with negative expecta-

tions. This attitude projects the message:
"I am unapproachable and unfriendly. Stay away from me."

Say, *"STOP!"* to this nonsense and START your tender self-talk:
"I love myself, and I love meeting women. I'm going to have a great time."

This tender thought helps you to walk in with positive expectations and project the message:
"I am approachable and friendly."

With this tender thought, you're off to a terrific start!

Walk up to the hostess

When you arrive at a party, walk up to the hostess. Because she wants you to have a good time, she will do her best to make you feel more at ease. If you don't know anyone, and you are feeling especially shy about approaching women, tell her. She will probably take you around the room and introduce you to several women.

Bring a buddy

The most relaxing way to make contact with a woman is to be introduced to her by someone else. Let your friend be your spokeswoman, and talk up your great qualities to other women. We are generally more bold introducing a friend than introducing ourselves. So, even if there is a woman you want to meet and neither of you know her, have your buddy introduce herself and then introduce *you*. Do the same thing for your friend. *Try it;* it's fun.

Get close

> *"I was at a club when I noticed a very attractive woman standing by the bar. I casually walked to the bar, stood about a foot away from her, and ordered a drink. After a few minutes, she looked at me. I smiled; she smiled. I said, 'Hi,' and we started talking. I had a terrific night."*

How is a woman going to notice you if you are hiding in a corner across the room?

To get her to notice you, you must get near her. If you see a woman you want to meet, start moving toward her. Create close, but not intrusive, physical proximity by standing near her, sitting by her, or joining her in an activity. Each step you take improves your contact chances.

111

Look and listen

Before approaching a woman, look at and listen to her. You are trying to figure out if she is friendly and receptive. Does she appear happy, sad, angry, or scared? We can never know for certain what a person's body language and facial expressions mean. For example, a very insecure woman may actually turn away from another woman to whom she is attracted. But, if you patiently observe a woman for a while, you're sure to get some insight into her emotional state.

Look, listen, and, in the end, go with your gut. Unless you are *certain* a woman isn't friendly, *assume* she is, and go up to her.

Make eye contact

Direct and strong eye contact is a powerful way of capturing a woman's attention. It's a clear gesture of interest, friendly or romantic. If you see a woman you would like to meet, catch her eye and hold it for a couple of seconds. This preliminary contact makes the next contact, introducing yourself to her, easier.

Good eye contact is not about staring. A woman may interpret staring as either intrusive or threatening. Glance rather than glare. Think positive, caring thoughts while you look at her, and she will realize that you want to meet her.

What is the best kind of eye contact to offer a

woman who can't look you in the eye? A woman may be so nervous that she is looking everywhere except at you. To ease her anxiety, gently make eye contact in a caring and inviting way. Don't ogle her as this may scare her into silence. Be sensitive and open, and she will almost always return the kindness.

What is the best way to make eye contact?

1. Look for a few seconds.

2. Look away for a minute.

3. Do this several times. If she doesn't respond to you right away, don't give up. What you assume is her lack of interest may be her lack of awareness; something or someone may be distracting her. She may also be unsure if you are making eye contact with her. She may be thinking, *"Is she looking at me or my friend?"* or, *"Was she intentionally looking at me, or just looking around the room?"* Be patient; keep trying to establish contact with her.

4. If she realizes you are making eye contact with her, and she returns your gaze, flash her a smile. Nothing communicates friendship and openness more than a big, heartfelt smile.

   Don't wait for her to come to you, go to her. She may be quite shy even though she glanced back at you. Walk over, and introduce yourself.

INTRODUCING YOURSELF

Deep down, most of us aren't unfriendly, only scared. We want so much to make contact with each other, but we aren't quite sure how to do it. The best way to introduce yourself is to be your best self, your loving self. A positive attitude, an open heart, direct eye contact, a warmhearted smile, a firm yet gentle handshake, and a cheerful greeting are the tools of an ideal introduction.

Be friendly

- ◆ Practice tender self-talk: *"I love myself, and I love meeting women"*
- ◆ Make direct eye contact; smile warmly; project positive energy.
- ◆ Have a relaxed stance; uncross those arms.

These behaviors communicate:
"I am friendly; I am approachable."

Do *everything* you can to encourage women to muster the courage to come up to you. Make sure your thoughts, facial expressions, and body language all signal friendliness.

Shake her hand

Shaking hands is, ordinarily, the first physical contact you have with a woman. Because this small nonverbal gesture communicates interest or disinterest, show a woman how happy you are to meet her by offering your hand with a warmhearted attitude.

Clasp her hand with your whole palm, not just the fingers, and don't give either a wimpy or a knuckle-breaking handshake. Too loose a grip signals insecurity; too tight a grip indicates aggression. A firm yet gentle handshake expresses self-confidence and sincerity.

Play the "name-game"

Remembering a woman's name is an extremely important social skill. It indicates that we are interested in and paying attention to the person we are meeting.

When a woman forgets our name, we think she is saying:

> *"You're not important to me."*
>
> *"I wasn't impressed enough with you to remember your name."*

Don't make that same mistake; we are all sensitive about our name.

However, sometimes we may forget a woman's name immediately after being introduced to her, as well as after not seeing her for a long time. Don't despair. Forgetting a name is nothing more than a bad habit. No one has a "bad" memory; we merely have bad memory habits.

The following is a quick lesson on good memory habits and how to teach yourself to remember names.

Use the *"STOP!"* and START technique:

Say, *"STOP!"* to the toxic self-talk telling you how awful you are at remembering names and START your tender self-talk:
"It's easy for me to remember names."
"I'm always at ease when I meet women."

Pay close attention. Failure to pay close attention to a woman's name when it is first said is the biggest reason for our inability to remember it.

Clear your mind. The greater your concentration, the greater your ability to retain a name. Learn to listen despite inner and outer distractions.

Look directly at the woman you're meeting and relate her face to her name. This establishes a powerful visual cue and helps you to retrieve her name from your memory when you see her face.

Create a deep mental impression of a name by listening carefully to the sound of it. Then, immediately repeat the name out-loud:

"Nice to meet you, ____."

Saying a woman's name aloud helps you to recall it more easily. Using this auditory cue also builds a rapport as it demonstrates interest.

Repeat the name silently to yourself. Repetition is necessary to implant a name into your memory. You can easily say a name silently to yourself while continuing a conversation.

Imagine a woman's name emblazoned on her forehead in red ink. The next time you see her face, you will "see" her name in bright red ink across her forehead.

Determine a woman's most descriptive personality or physical trait. Then, using the same first letter as her first name, pick an adjective which describes the trait. For example, "Funny Fran," "Tall Tanya,"

"Sexy Samantha." This will help to imprint her name into your mind.

What do you do if you forget a woman's name? The best thing to do is to confess your faux pas: *"I'm so sorry; I forgot your name. Please forgive me, and tell me your name again."*

When she tells you her name, again, be sure to use all of the name remembering skills you have learned.

Introduce women to each other

Never lose an opportunity to introduce women to each other. It's not only polite, it's smart; they will, in turn, introduce you to their friends. The best introductions are enthusiastic and tell women what they have in common. A mutual interest is an instant subject for discussion.

Making contact with a woman who is alone

"Whenever I go to a party where I don't know many women, I look for the women who are standing or sitting alone. They always welcome my company."

While touring your surroundings, notice the women who are alone. They are probably as nervous

118

as you are. These women are the easiest to approach as they greatly appreciate the contact. Show your self-confidence and sincerity by walking right up to a woman who is alone, looking her in the eye, smiling broadly, extending your hand, and warmly saying, *"Hi!"*

Before saying, *"Hi,"* say, *"STOP!"* to your toxic self-talk:

"What if I walk up to her, say, 'Hi,' and she ignores me? It's not worth taking the risk; forget about it."

START your tender self-talk:

"I love myself, and I love meeting women."

"I make contact easily with the women I want to meet."

How do you sound when you say, *"Hi"*? Bored? Anxious? Depressed? Happy? Enthusiastic? Practice· putting positive energy into your greeting—you want it to be gracious and inviting. Let your loving self shine through your salutation, and you will be warmly received.

Making contact with a group

"Sometimes, I will be at a party, and there will be a group of women who are laughing and having fun. They all seem to know each other. I would like to be included in their group, but

I feel uncomfortable joining in unless I am invited."

You see a group of women who look like they're having fun, and you want to become a part of it. What do you do? Many of us feel intimidated and do nothing. Don't fret. This isn't the impenetrable situation you may think it is. With equal amounts of courage and sensitivity, you can successfully join groups of women.

Before you approach a group of women, say, "*STOP!*" to your toxic self-talk:

"I'll look like an idiot if I try to join this group. They don't want to include me. They aren't interested in talking to me."

START your tender self-talk:

"I'm a pleasure to know; I'm always welcomed wherever I go. It's easy for me to join a group."

I use the word "join" rather than "break into" deliberately. "Join" implies inclusion while "break into" implies exclusion. You want to *include* yourself in a group, not intrude upon it.

Stand on the periphery of a group you wish to join. Look at and listen to the women:

▼ Are they involved in an intense or a light, playful discussion?

▼ Are they seriously engaged with each other, or merely hanging out?

▼ Are they looking only at each other or checking out the scene?

▼ Is the energy exclusive or inclusive?

Pay attention and use your intuition. If you conclude that the women aren't engaged in a private conversation, and that they seem sociable, show interest by looking at each of the women in the group and by giving appropriate feedback to what is being said: Nod, smile, laugh.

Interrupting a woman mid-sentence to announce your entrance into the group is *not* a smart way to ask to be included. Wait for a pause in the group conversation; patience is critical to joining groups successfully.

When you sense a lull, make yourself a part of the group by walking up to it and facing the women. Introduce yourself *to the group* by looking at each woman, smiling warmly, and saying, *"Hi!"* Then, introduce yourself *to each woman*.

If the group is too large to introduce yourself to all at once, wait for a break in the conversation, walk up to a woman in the group and, say, *"Hello."*

Another way to join a group involves overhearing a question to which no one in the group seems to know the answer. If this happens, offer an answer and then, naturally, introduce yourself.

After introducing yourself, pay attention to *every* woman in the group. Make an effort to connect, if only for a moment, with each woman. A good social skills rule is to always pay some attention to everyone you encounter. It's common courtesy.

Sometimes, a group will not want you to join it. If your attempts to be included are ignored, don't take it personally.

Say, *"STOP!"* to any toxic self-talk and START your tender self-talk:

"I'm proud of myself for facing my fear of rejection by attempting to make contact with a group of women."

With your self-esteem intact, go find more cordial women.

If a woman wants to join *your* group, be generous with her. It probably took her a long time to gather her nerve to approach your group. Recall your discomfort in similar situations, and warmly welcome her.

Making contact with a particular woman who is not alone

"I don't approach a woman if she is with other women because I feel intimidated. I always wait until she is alone. If she is never alone, I never go up to her. Sad, but true."

If you want to make contact with a particular woman who is not alone, consider the questions discussed in the "Making contact with a group" section.

In addition, determine if there are obvious signs of romance between the woman you want to meet and any of the other women.

When it comes to making contact, I believe in erring on the *other* side of caution. Unless you are *certain* she is with a lover, assume she isn't and walk up to the *women* and say, *"Hello."*

After chatting with each woman, subtly position yourself next to the woman you're attracted to and start asking her some questions about herself. (We'll go into this in more detail in Chapter Six, "Talking.")

Another way to initiate contact is to write your first name, home phone number and something cheerful on a piece of paper:

> *"You have a beautiful smile. I don't want to interrupt you and your friends; I'd love to meet you when you're available. Please call me."*

Walk up to her, establish eye contact, smile, and say:

> *"Excuse me, I want to give this to you. Enjoy your night."*

Then, turn and walk away. The woman you approached will be pleased by your assertive (and polite) attention. And who knows? She may call you.

Making contact with a woman who is dancing

You spot a woman who is dancing, and you want

to meet her. What do you do, besides continuing to watch her?

The most unobtrusive way to get close enough to make contact is by dancing, with a friend, near her. This will also give you a chance to evaluate the relationship between her and her dance partner.

After you've concluded that the two of them are probably not lovers, face the woman you want to meet, establish eye contact and flash her a broad smile. If she returns your gaze and smiles, chances are she is interested in meeting you. So, introduce yourself to her and her dance partner, and introduce both of them to your dance partner. And don't forget to compliment yourself for being so fearlessly assertive. You're doing great!

Making contact with other couples

Making contact with other couples is similar to making contact with single women. Be assertive and affable. When you do meet another interesting lesbian couple, don't be reticent. Suggest exchanging phone numbers and getting together for dinner. Don't wait for them to call you. Take the initiative and call them to set up a double-date.

Friendships are no different from romantic relationships. It takes time and effort to turn strangers into friends. Make the call, and you *will* make a friend.

"ARE THEY TOGETHER OR JUST FRIENDS?"

"I'm nervous about asking a woman to dance, and being told the woman standing next to her is her girlfriend. I have a hard time figuring out if two women are lovers or friends. I think single women should wear shirts saying, 'Single.'"

I love many things about being a lesbian. Playing the infamous lesbian guessing game, "Are They Together or Just Friends?" is not one of them. It can be very frustrating trying to figure out the relationship between two women. Some friends are affectionate with each other. Some lovers aren't.

Too many of us are reluctant to approach a woman because of this issue. Don't be afraid! It's always better to take a risk and find out a woman is with her girlfriend, then to do nothing and lose the chance to meet a terrific woman.

Most of us are so terrified of rejection that we actually look for reasons not to reach out to each other. If there is the *slightest* chance two women are lovers, most women will not approach either of them. This passive behavior is not about respect, but about fear. Don't let the fear of making contact with someone else's girlfriend stop you from introducing yourself.

If you ask a woman to dance—good for you!—, and she says, *"No, I'm here with my lover,"* don't get flustered.

Simply smile, and say:

"Sorry to have bothered you; enjoy your night."

Say, *"STOP!"* to any toxic thoughts, and START your tender self-talk:

"I'm proud of myself for having made the effort to make contact with another woman. Good for me!"

A few years ago, at a dance club in New York City, I asked a woman to dance, and she turned me down because the woman standing by her side, who I thought was a platonic friend, was her lover. About five minutes after I asked this unavailable woman to dance, she came over to me and introduced me to her friend. The friend and I hit it off, and we danced all night. Now that is what social networking is all about!

I learned an invaluable making contact lesson that night. As long as I am respectful whenever I approach a woman, it's *impossible* for me to make an unforgivable mistake.

CONTACT WINNERS

- Being assertive
- Making direct eye contact
- Smiling broadly
- Participating in activities
- Having a relaxed posture
- Offering a firm yet gentle handshake
- Introducing yourself with a spirited, *"Hi!"*
- Standing or sitting in the middle of the action
- Volunteering

Chapter Six

Talking

"We are what we repeatedly do. Excellence, then, is not an act, but a habit."
—Aristotle

"WHAT DO I SAY NOW?"

You see a woman you would like to meet. You observe her body language, facial expressions, and interactions with others. Your "expert" conclusion: She seems friendly and available.

Having promised yourself you would introduce yourself to at least one new woman tonight, you take one more gulp of your bottled water and start walking toward her.

As you get close to her, you establish direct eye contact, offer an affable smile, extend your hand, and say:

"Hi, I'm ____."

What do you say now?

BUILDING A RAPPORT

The techniques presented in this chapter will help you to start, continue, and end conversations confidently and easily. I offer them *not* as a bunch of tricks with which to manipulate women, but as a bounty of goodwill with which to build a rapport with women. Rapport is an emotional connection or bond. It is the heart and soul of all successful conversations and relationships. When a rapport is developed, we feel comfortable with, close to, and trusting of each other.

How do you establish this affinity with another woman?

By genuinely caring about her.

The following tools of talk will help you to show that you genuinely care.

BEING SINCERELY INTERESTED

> *"There are no uninteresting things,*
> *only uninterested people."*
> —Anonymous

Being sincerely interested in a woman is the path to having a great conversation with her. When you show a woman you care about who she is and what she has to say, she will want to talk with you.

Every woman is a unique person with immeasurable knowledge, talents, and life experiences; be open to discovering her. Treat every conversation as a valuable learning opportunity.

If you are sincerely interested in a woman, she will appreciate your desire to learn about her. You're always the most interesting *to* her when you're the most interested *in* her.

PAYING ATTENTION

Paying close attention to a speaker shows your commitment to the conversation. A woman will interpret your unfaltering focus as a clear sign that you're interested in her, and this will endear you to her.

130

Don't let yourself get distracted with someone or something else. If you do, you will not be able to give your full attention. This may cause the woman you're speaking with to conclude that you don't care about her.

Also, don't let yourself get distracted with *yourself*. When you first start talking with a woman, you may be concerned about making a good impression. You may feel anxious because you're concentrating on what you want to *get* (attention, approval, etc.) from a conversation. Concentrate on what you can *give* (attention, appreciation, etc.), and any anxiety will disappear. Conversational fears will always diminish when you focus on being interested *in* her rather than being interesting *to* her.

LISTEN ACTIVELY

Do you know how to listen actively?

Active listening is *not* the opposite of talking. Just because someone isn't speaking doesn't automatically mean she is intently listening. It's also not the same thing as hearing (or passively listening). You may be physically present, but you are not paying close attention to what is being said. Active listening demands concentration and commitment because your mind and emotions are engaged in the conversation.

Active listening is fundamental to great conversation because your interest and appreciation encourages the speaker to keep talking. It tells the speaker that, for the moment, you think she is the most important person in the world.

To be an active listener, you must, first, want to listen. Clear your mind of your own agenda, and concentrate on the speaker. You will not listen well if you fixate on what you want to *get* out of a conversation; you will listen well if you focus on what you can *give* to the conversation.

Be sure to *show* a woman you're attentively listening to her. A speaker always looks for acknowledgments from her listener. She wants to know she is being listened to and understood.

Here are some ways to tell the speaker:

"I'm listening and I understand; please keep talking."

1. Send *verbal* "keep talking" acknowledgments.

   Many women interpret a listener's total silence as a sign of boredom or disinterest. Sounds of encouragement let a speaker know the listener is actively listening.

   These small noises give a woman the go-ahead to continue speaking:

"Hmmm."

"How interesting."

"Uh-huh."

"Yes."

"I see."

"Is that so?"

"I understand."

"Go on."

"Tell me more."

"I get it."

Paraphrase (restate in other words) what a woman says to you. This is another way to let her know you are carefully listening, you understand, and you want her to keep talking.

2. Send *non-verbal* "keep talking" acknowledgments.

Our non-verbal communications (tone of voice, facial expressions, and body language) send powerful messages to either keep talking or stop talking. We may be unaware of how a speaker deciphers our tone, face, and body.

A speaker will conclude you want her to keep talking if you …

Face her. Facing the speaker with your entire body lets her know you want to hear what she has to say and you're interested in her.

Maintain direct eye contact. This is an indication that you're intently listening to her. Keep the eye contact relaxed; it doesn't have to be constant to be effectual.

Looking straight into a woman's eyes as she speaks communicates understanding and interest and builds trust in you. By contrast, if you continuously look up, away, or over her shoulder to scope out the room for other women, you're communicating a lack of interest in her. A disrespect sure to create ill will. If you want to check out the scene without offending, politely excuse yourself.

Use other non-verbal acknowledgments; i.e., smiling, leaning forward, and nodding to communicate you're paying close attention.

If you listen actively, you will always have something to talk about—the more you listen, the more you learn about the speaker. And, the more you learn about her, the more relevant comments and questions you will be able to offer.

Give a woman a safe space in which to speak (by attentively listening to her and by being empathetic), and she will tell you about herself.

BEING EMPATHETIC

The essence of a rapport is empathy, and the core

134

of empathy is understanding. Empathy enables you to relate to another woman's experience of the world by "stepping into her shoes." You're empathetic—you understand how *she* feels—when you're able to see the world through *her* eyes and feel the world through *her* heart.

When you show you understand how a woman feels, she will feel understood. When both women in a conversation feel they understand and are understood by each other, a rapport is created.

When you listen with empathy, you listen not only with your ears but with your *heart*. You never judge or criticize. You solely acknowledge the feelings of another, without evaluation.

Empathetic listening conveys the message:

"I am listening, and I understand how you feel. I care about you."

When you don't practice empathetic listening, you listen with a critical ear; you judge and you advise:

"That's the wrong thing to do."

"You should do this."

"You shouldn't do that."

If a woman proudly tells you about a recent accomplishment, show your empathy by reflecting her emotion in your response:

"That's fantastic!"

This is an empathetic response because it recognizes

135

and validates feelings. Saying, *"Oh, that's nice."* will not create a rapport as such a tepid reaction doesn't adequately reflect the enthusiasm of your speaker.

With an empathetic response, the emphasis is on the *speaker's* feelings:

"You sound sad. I'm sorry you're in pain."

This reply *reflects* the speaker's emotions and *acknowledges* them.

With a non-empathetic response, the emphasis is on the *listener's* feelings:

"Why are you so upset? It's not a big deal."

This reply *analyzes* the speaker's emotions and *denies* them. We all crave to be listened to and understood, not fixed. This is why empathetic listening and responding forges such powerful emotional connections.

SMALL TALK

All relationships start with small talk; it's the first step toward getting to know someone. Small talk is simply a prop for starting a conversation; the substance of the conversation isn't as important as the act of conversing. The best small talk centers on non-threatening topics, such as, the immediate surroundings, a shared experience, or common knowledge.

Meeting someone new can throw us emotionally off-balance; we may feel anxious. Talking about innocuous things like the food, the party, or the weather helps us to regain our emotional balance. Through small talk we are able to warm up to each other and feel more at ease.

Small talk isn't supposed to be brilliant; it's supposed to be relaxing and engaging. Don't worry about trying to impress a woman with a profound remark. A pleasant comment, question, or compliment will draw her into a dialogue with you.

To get the most out of a casual conversation, fully participate in it. Commit to being thoroughly involved in a discussion, even if it lasts only a few minutes.

Small talking is a vital tool of talk. You can't have a relationship with a woman if you don't have a conversation with her, and small talk gets the conversational ball rolling.

Offer a comment, not an opening line

"I never know how to start a conversation with another woman. What do you talk about with someone you don't know? I usually wait for someone else to break the ice. But, often, no one does. Too bad I don't have any good opening lines."

The only good opening line is *no* opening line. Worn-out gambits are an absolute turn-off; don't use them. Instead, offer a relevant and positive comment. It's a perfect ice breaker because it's a friendly invitation to talk.

You can make a comment on what is happening around you, such as, the decor, the speaker, the event, the organization, the music, the paintings. Anything (and everything) you find interesting is a ready topic for breaking the ice.

Some possible comments:

> *"What a great club!"*
>
> *"What an interesting sculpture."*
>
> *"The music is terrific."*
>
> *"Wow, there are a lot of women here!"*
>
> *"What a perfect day to be at the beach!"*
>
> *"The food is delicious."*
>
> *"What a lovely home."*
>
> *"She's an excellent speaker."*
>
> *"This is a wonderful event"*
>
> *"That's a gorgeous painting."*

Stay away from negative comments:
"This is an awful party!"

Such remarks are alienating.

Ask a question

> *"I always stammer when first meeting a*

woman. I can never think of anything to say; it's as though my mind goes blank. Once we get the conversation going, I'm fine. But, until then, I sound like an idiot."

Another perfect ice breaker is a pertinent question because it stimulates interest. The question can be about anything going on around you. Take a good look at your surroundings; it will supply you with an ample number of conversational starters.

Remember, you're not asking a question to get information; you're asking a question to engage someone in conversation. A good question invites discussion. This is why an open-ended question (a question beginning with *"who," "what," "when," "where," "why,"* and *"how"*) is preferable to a closed-ended question (a question requesting a *"yes"* or *"no"* answer).

An open-ended question encourages a woman to talk. Make the question positive and non-intrusive. You don't want to make a woman feel uncomfortable with a question which is negative or too personal; she may become closed and defensive.

"What do you think about ...?" is a great question with which to strike up a conversation. Every woman enjoys being asked her opinion.

Asking an open-ended question shows a woman you *care* about what she thinks. This helps to forge a bond between the two of you.

Another benefit of asking an open-ended question is that it helps you to discover common ground.

Whenever you and another woman identify mutual interests and values, an emotional connection is created. We all like being around women who share our enthusiasms.

If you ask a closed-ended question, you will get a *"yes/no"* answer. Your question may be answered, but your interaction may also be over. Ask closed-ended questions to get information; ask open-ended questions to get a dialogue going:

Closed-ended questions	Open-ended questions
"Are you enjoying the party?" *"Do you like the exhibit?"* *"Did you like the performance?"* *"Are you a friend of the hostess?"*	*"What do you think about the party?"* *"What is your favorite piece in the exhibit?"* *"Who was your favorite performer?"* *"How do you know the hostess?"*

However, there are some open-ended questions which are conversational killers, such as:

> *"How are you?"*
> *"What's up?"*
> *"What's new?"*

These questions are not only vague, their overuse has virtually stripped them of all meaning. Likely answers you'll hear are, *"Fine"* and *"Not much."* The conversation dies, right in front of you.

> *"Talk to people about themselves and they will listen for hours."*
>
> —Disraeli

Once you're over the initial hurdle of breaking the ice, the best way to keep the dialogue going is to discover topics about which a woman is impassioned.

You do this by continuing to ask open-ended questions:

Question: *"What do you do?"*
Answer: *"I'm an attorney."*
Question: *"What do you enjoy about practicing law?"*
Answer: *"Not much."*
Question: *"What do you love to do?"*
Answer: *"What do you mean?"*
Question: *"What do you do for fun? What activities bring you joy?"*
Answer: *"Well, I love to play golf. I play as often as possible. Sometimes, I think I work merely to pay my green fees. I'm going to golf school for two weeks this summer. I got a new set of ..."*

Golf is this woman's "on button." She could go on and on about golf because it's one of her favorite subjects. If you like golf, you will have hit upon a common interest. If you don't like golf, attentively listen to her for a while (view this as an opportunity to learn more about golf) and then casually introduce a topic about which you are more excited.

Although posing open-ended questions is a great way to build a rapport with a woman, firing off a barrage of questions is not. She will probably feel ill at ease with such excessive attention. Be respectfully curious, not intrusive.

Pay a compliment

A compliment is also a great ice breaker. Every woman appreciates genuine praise because it lets her know someone cares enough to notice her:

"I noticed your hat. It's beautiful, and it looks great on you."

But, I suggest you don't follow-up this compliment with:

"Where can I get one?"

A woman may be offended by this question because when you ask, *"Where can I get one?"* you are no longer concerned with her, but with yourself. Let a woman know you are interested in her by focusing your compliment *solely* on her.

The best compliments are specific and sincere. Ask yourself:

"What do I genuinely find attractive about her?"

"What do I genuinely admire about her?"

It could be anything: her paintings, a jacket, a hat, her speech ... When you figure out what you like about her, pay her an honest compliment:

"I thoroughly enjoyed your show; you were very funny."

Personalizing a compliment also makes a woman feel special—

Don't say: *"That's a great jacket."*

Do say: *"That jacket looks great on you."*

Be aware that a compliment is different than flattery. When you flatter a woman, you talk about who she is:

"You're a terrific speaker."

Flattering a woman is a poor way to start a conversation as she may interpret this as insincere praise. We all have built-in insincerity detectors. To ensure that your compliment is seen as the authentic admiration that it is, praise a woman for what she *does*, not for who she is:

"I really enjoyed your speech; I was deeply moved by it."

Also, flattery can leave a woman asking, *"Why?"* It may be unclear to her as to why you are compli-

143

menting her, and if she is puzzled by your praise, she may doubt your integrity. When you tell her what you appreciate about her, the compliment— and your authenticity—will be clearly perceived.

WHEN AND HOW TO BREAK THE ICE

"I never know how and when to start a conversation with another woman. I always feel unsure of myself."

Beginning a conversation with someone we don't know can be difficult. Choosing a good time and place is very important.

How many times have you gone to a dance club or event and seen a line to get inside? Is there ever not a line at the bar or the bathroom? These are good opportunities to make contact and talk with other women.

Before you do anything, remind yourself that every time you work on your social skills, you work on overcoming your fear of rejection.

Say, *"STOP!"* to any toxic self-talk and START your tender self-talk:

"I love myself, and I love meeting women. I start enjoyable conversations with women easily."

Social Scene:
You're waiting at the bar, trying to get a drink. You notice a woman standing next to you, by herself, waiting to place her drink order.

Establish eye contact, smile, and make a comment, ask a question, or pay her a compliment—

A comment:
"Wow, I can't believe how crowded it is tonight!"

A question:
"What time is the singer going on stage?"

A compliment:
"I noticed your hat; it looks great on you."

Social Scene:
You're waiting in line for the ladies room with twenty other women (of course). You hear two women behind you talking about the great food at this event.

Turn around, look each woman in the eye, smile, and try a comment, then a question:
"I couldn't help hearing you talk about the food. Everything is so delicious. What's your favorite dish?"

Making a comment on something you overhear is a perfectly acceptable way to break the ice. Naturally, if you overhear something personal, don't comment on it—you don't want to seem intrusive, only interested. Noticing is appreciated; prying is resented.

After you have been talking for a few minutes, introduce yourself.

In both of these examples, you may attempt to have a conversation with a woman who doesn't want to speak with you. If this happens, say, *"STOP!"* to any toxic self-talk and START your tender self-talk:

"I'm so proud of myself for reaching out."

Then, go find someone else more sociable.

TAKING TURNS

It's no fun being around a woman who always talks and never listens. She monopolizes a conversation with non-stop tales of her life, alienating everyone around her. It's also no fun being around a woman who refuses to be forthcoming with any personal information.

Show a woman how much you enjoy talking with her by asking her open-ended questions about herself and her life. In addition, be open about who you are and what you think when she asks about you and your life. Sharing yourself makes a woman feel more at ease about sharing herself. If both of you can feel relaxed enough to be vulnerable with each other, you will create an effortless rapport.

When asked, talk about your beliefs and your passions. Then, relate what you are saying back to your conversational partner. You can easily do this by following up a remark about yourself with a question about her:

> *"And, what about you?"*
>
> *"What is your opinion on that?"*
>
> *"How do you feel about that?"*

The ideal conversation, one which is emotionally satisfying to both women, is akin to a ping-pong game, the object of which is to keep the conversational ball moving back and forth for as long as possible. Both of you are talking and listening, happily going from one topic to the next.

INTERRUPTION

Most of us dislike being interrupted when we speak. Give the speaker all the time she needs to complete her thought. Regardless of your enthusiasm for a subject, resist the impulse to interrupt her.

BEING RIGHT

"If I do not believe as you believe, and you do not believe as I believe, all it shows is that I don't believe as you believe and you don't believe as I believe."

—Emerson

If you want to be a successful conversationalist, it is important not to argue with a speaker. This may seem obvious, but I'm sure you can recall speaking with someone who had to be right and make everyone else wrong. Contentious women do not easily make or keep friends.

You don't have to *agree* with everything a woman says; you only need to *listen* respectfully. Rather than telling someone she is wrong, allow her to have her beliefs, without condescending commentary. Reasonable women can differ; *both* of you can be right at the same time.

Use one of these "acknowledgment expressions" the next time someone says something with which you disagree:

"I appreciate what you're saying, and I think ..."

"I respect what you're saying, and I think ..."

"I understand what you're saying, and I think ..."

Notice I have intentionally used the word, "and" instead of, "but." "But" makes the speaker *wrong* while "and" *acknowledges* her. Make it a point never to tell someone she is wrong. This is a cardinal rule of successful conversation.

GIVING ADVICE

Giving advice is one of the fastest ways to kill a conversation. No one likes being told what to do. Listen; don't fix. Women who play "Ms. Fix-it" offer unsolicited advice and solutions. Their comments usually begin with, *"You should ..."* "Should" may be the most offensive word in the English language, because it deprives us of choice. Respect a woman enough to let her find her own solutions.

If your advice is asked for, proceed with caution. Give advice sparingly. Remember, no one likes to be told she is wrong. Frame any advice in terms of what you *would* do in her position, not what she *should* do: *"If I were you, I would ..."*

Because you're not telling her what to do, you're not telling her she is wrong if she decides to ignore your way of handling a situation. You can both be right even though your opinions may differ.

FILLER WORDS AND PHRASES

Many of us use filler words and phrases, such as, *"you know," "like," "um,"* and *"uh."* We use these verbal tics to give our brain time to catch up with our mouth. Using these expressions is a bad habit that detracts from effective communication.

The first step toward breaking this habit is to become aware of how many times you use these words. Pay attention to the words you use, and you might be surprised how often they pop up.

To become a better speaker, pay close attention to your speech patterns. Slow down. You won't need to use filler words and phrases if you choose your words with care.

SPEAK CLEARLY

Mumbling makes it difficult for a listener to understand you. It may also be an indication of low self-esteem. If you want to make a good impression and have a woman enjoy talking with you, speak clearly, audibly, and with warmth.

BREATHE

When you feel particularly tense, your heart may pound, and you may get short of breath. This physiological response occurs because adrenaline is surging through your body. To calm yourself down, all you have to do is breathe deeply. Breathe in through your mouth for three seconds, hold for three seconds, and breathe out through your mouth for three seconds. Do this several times, and you will begin to relax.

PREPARATION

Before you get into a social situation, think about what you might like to talk about with a conversational partner.

Here are various suggestions for cultivating interesting topics for discussion:

▼ Read local and national lesbian and gay publications.

▼ Stay abreast of current events.

▼ Watch movies and television shows.

▼ Read books, especially those with lesbian themes.

▼ When attending a political meeting, fund-raising party, or other event, be informed on the organization's work and some of its activities.

PRACTICE MAKES PERFECT

> *"Perfection is attained by slow degrees;*
> *she requires the hand of time."*
> —Voltaire

Practicing your talking skills will help you to feel

more confident about your talking abilities. Practice whenever and with whomever you can: when jogging; when looking in the mirror; with your cat; with your friends; with your therapist ...

ASKING FOR A DATE

"I don't know if it's a date. We were on the phone for over an hour, and we agreed to get together Thursday evening for dinner. Neither one of us used the word "date." Is it a date if you make plans to get together during the week? If we had made plans for Saturday night, I'm pretty sure that would qualify as a date, I think. What do you think?"

I think the whole thing is *crazy*. This is the classic lesbian dating dilemma.

In the heterosexual community, when a man asks to "get together" with a woman (or a woman asks a man), it is generally understood that a date is being made. It's not so clear in our community because we often pursue friendships with one another. The solution to the *"I don't know if it's a date"* problem is simple: Find out if it's a date *before* you get together.

Social Scene:
You're at a benefit auction for a lesbian organization. You meet an attractive woman, and the two of you have had a great time

talking. You decide that you want to go on a date with her. But, you're reluctant to bring up the topic in such a crowded environment. Instead, you would rather exchange phone numbers so you can ask her, in private, for a date.

What do you do?

Tell her that you enjoyed your conversation and you would like to exchange phone numbers. Don't let your fear of rejection steal your voice.

If she agrees, call her—*when* you want to call her. Some women fear if they don't wait three days before calling someone, they will appear needy or desperate. As long as you don't *feel* needy or desperate, why mindlessly subscribe to this arbitrary rule?

Before you call, practice your tender self-talk:

"I'm a woman of worth. It's easy for me to ask a woman for a date."

Whenever we are reluctant to ask a woman for a date, it's because we don't want to hear the dreaded word, *"No."* Remind yourself that no matter what happens, you're still a wonderful woman, and if she says, *"No,"* all it means is that she isn't for you. It doesn't mean you aren't attractive, charming, intelligent, desirable, or anything else.

When you do call, remind her of who you are. Be honest with her about your desire to date her. Being honest saves time, energy, and aggravation. It also builds your self-esteem. Whenever you tell someone who you are and what you want, you are taking good care of yourself by validating your feelings.

Refer to your conversation at the event where you met her, small talk for a while, and then, say:

"I really enjoyed meeting you, and I'd like to go on a date with you. Are you available for dinner next Friday or Saturday night?"

Design the date *before* you call. She will appreciate the obvious thought you put into planning your first date.

Don't make the mistake of being vague. Rather than saying, *"Do you want to go on a date some time?"* be *specific* when extending an invitation.

For example:

"Do you want to go on a date for dinner next Tuesday or Wednesday evening?"

"Would you like to go on a date to see a movie next Sunday night?"

Let her propose *alternatives* to your plan, but make sure you *have* a plan.

Asking a woman for a date is a very personal matter—use whatever words feel right to you. The most important thing to remember is to *always* tell the truth about your feelings; it's also a good idea to speak in *"I"* statements:

"I really enjoyed meeting you."

"I had a great time."

"I'd like to go on a date with you."
"I think you're terrific."

Regardless of the outcome, give yourself a big pat on the back for risking rejection in such a fearless manner. Good for you! If she wants to date you, fine. If not, that's also fine. If she tells you she doesn't want to date you but she does want to be your friend, take time to think about whether this is good for you. You don't have to be friends with a woman you're interested in dating.

EXIT GRACEFULLY

"I'm always uncomfortable when I want to end a conversation and talk with someone else. I don't want to hurt a woman's feelings, but some women get your ear and won't let go. I never know what to say."

Ending conversations can cause anxiety if you don't know how to do it skillfully. Whether you're having an enjoyable dialogue with a woman, or not, here are effective and courteous ways to exit gracefully:

◆ If you enjoyed your conversation, and you want to speak with her again later—

155

Look her in the eye, smile, extend your hand and say:
"It's been great talking with you. I need to speak with someone else, but I'd love to talk with you again before you leave."

If she returns your enthusiasm, agree to find each other before you leave. If she doesn't positively respond to your proposal, smile and say:
"No problem; enjoy the rest of your evening."

Be sure to congratulate yourself for fighting your fear by extending an invitation.

◆ If you don't want to speak with her later, you could say—

"It's been nice speaking with you; have a good time."
"I'm going to circulate; enjoy yourself."

Don't let your fear of hurting a woman's feelings keep you in a conversation which you're not enjoying. It's your responsibility to take care of yourself. It isn't your responsibility to take care of her. That's *her* responsibility. Be caring; don't be caretaking. Honesty coupled with compassion is always the best policy.

SAYING, "NO"

> "I have a hard time turning a woman down. I don't want to hurt her feelings. I've actually dated women I didn't want to date because I couldn't bring myself to say, "'No.'"

What is the best way to decline an invitation?

Many women tell me of their discomfort with saying, "No" to a woman they don't want to date. Once again, honesty coupled with compassion is the best policy:

> "No, thank you, but it's nice of you to ask."
>
> "I appreciate you asking, but no, thank you."
>
> "I appreciate the invitation, but I'm not interested in going on a date."

If a woman you're not interested in dating tells you that she wants to get together with you, and you aren't sure if her intentions are friendly or romantic, ask her:

> "Is this a date?"

If she says, "Yes," say:

> "I appreciate the invitation, but I'm not interested in going on a date."

If you want to get together as friends, be forewarned. It might be better to end a friendship before it begins if a woman you don't want to date has a romantic interest in you. And, it isn't fair to a woman who wants to date you if you don't tell her that you don't feel the same way. Tell her how you feel, and allow her to decide if she wants to spend any more time with you.

If you do want to be friends with her, you may be reluctant to tell her your true platonic feelings out of fear that she will not want to be your friend. I believe *this* is the reason many of us aren't truthful with each other around this issue. The problem is that unless you change your mind—or she changes her feelings—she will eventually resent you.

I have seen one disaster after another because women were not truthful with each other about what they wanted. Being totally honest with others, as well as yourself, is the only route to having loving and trusting relationships.

TO KEEP A CONVERSATION GOING ...

- Be sincerely interested
- Pay close attention
- Listen actively and with empathy
- Offer genuine praise
- Make comments
- Maintain direct eye contact
- Speak clearly
- Ask open-ended questions
- Directly face your conversational partner
- Use other non-verbal acknowledgments

Chapter Seven

Social Security

*"Do the thing you fear the most
and the death of fear is certain."*
—Emerson

You now have the psychological tools to construct a good sense of self as well as the practical techniques for effective meeting and greeting. Together, these skills will help you to meet the women you want to meet confidently and easily.

You are ready for the final strategy to use in your battle against the fear of rejection: You must *risk rejection!* To overcome fear, any fear, you must face it. Thoughts of self-love, acts of self-love, sufficient preparation, and repeated exposure to that which you fear are the magical combination which signal the end of fear.

Let's fashion a hypothetical social scene in which to practice your women-meeting skills:

> Imagine you're at a large, boisterous party. You have been talking with several new women to whom you have been introduced. So far, so good. Here comes the big test: You spot an adorable woman engaged in what appears to be a lively discussion with several friends. You definitely want to meet her.

Your toxic self-talk begins:
"I want to go up to her and introduce myself. I can't do that; I'll make a fool of myself. She's with a bunch of friends. I'm sure she doesn't want to talk to me. Even if she does, I don't know what to say."

You refuse to remain a victim to your toxic tapes ...

1. You take a deep breath.

2. You say, *"STOP!"* to your toxic self-talk, and you START your tender self-talk:

   "I love myself, and I love meeting women."
   "I am a woman of worth."
   "I easily make contact and talk with women."

   You silently repeat these affirmations to yourself.

3. You casually move closer to the group, close enough to be able to look at the women and listen to their conversation. You're trying to find out if the discussion is private, and if the woman you want to meet is there with her girlfriend. Knowing that body language is tough to trust, you don't read too much into it.

4. You continue to look and listen. The conversation seems light: The women are smiling and laughing. You notice no obvious signs of romance. Instead, the women, including the one you're interested in, all appear to be friends, engag-

ing in conversation and keeping an eye on what's happening around them. You conclude that the group's energy is friendly and inclusive.

5. When someone in the group makes a joke, you nod, smile, and make eye contact with as many of the women as possible. When the next lull in the conversation occurs, you look at each woman, smile, and introduce yourself.

6. After introductions, you deftly lob the conversational ball over the net by asking the group an open-ended question: *"What do you think about the party?"*

   You keep the conversation flowing, following up their responses with questions that invite them to keep talking.

7. Although you're having a lot of fun talking with the entire group, you specifically want to speak one-on-one with the woman you find so adorable. You subtly position yourself next to her, and start asking her some questions about herself: *"What do you do?"* *"What do you love to do?"*

Because you want to develop a rapport with her, you do everything you can to let her know you are interested in her and what she is saying. For instance, you communicate that you are actively listening to her by smiling, nodding, and offering supportive and germane remarks.

8. When she asks you about yourself, you continue to build your rapport by openly sharing yourself. You reveal your vulnerability by speaking honestly about your beliefs and interests. You then switch the conversational spotlight back to her by asking:

"What are your feelings about this?"
"What do you think about that?"

9. The other women in the group want to dance. You and your new friend are asked to join them, but you both decide to stay where you are and keep talking. Your lively dialogue continues until at last it is interrupted by her friends, who mention that it's getting late and they want to leave. You look at your watch and are surprised that it's after midnight. The two of you have been talking for over an hour!

10. Knowing that you want to speak with her again, you say:
"I had a great time talking with you, and I'd love to continue our conversation. Do you want to exchange numbers?"

She responds positively to your invitation.

11. Because you want to ask her on a date, you plan the date before you call her. You recall her telling you how much she enjoys movies. You decide to ask her to go see the new lesbian movie opening next weekend.

12. You call her when you want to call her, two days later. Before you dial her number, you say, *"STOP!"* to any toxic self-talk:
"What if she turns me down? I'll be so embarrassed. Maybe, I won't call her. It might be better to wait for her to call me."

You START your tender self-talk:
"I am a woman of worth; it's easy for me to ask a woman on a date."

When you speak with her, you remind her of who you are and where you met her, and you chat for a while.

Then, you say:
"I really enjoyed meeting you, and I'd like to go on a date with you. Are you interested in seeing the new lesbian movie with me next Friday night?"

13. She tells you she isn't available next Friday night. She asks if you want to go out Saturday night instead. Saturday night is fine for you, so you both agree as to a time and a place to meet.

    The two of you speak a few minutes longer, and you finish up the phone call by saying:
    "I'm sure Saturday night will be fun; I'm looking forward to seeing you."

    You say good-bye and congratulate yourself for valiantly pushing through your fear of rejection by asking her for a date.

You may be thinking this little story is a fairy tale, and things don't happen this smoothly in real life. Maybe this will happen instead:

1. After you tell her you want to date her, she tells you:
   "Thanks for asking, but I'm not interested in going on a date. If you want to get together as friends, that would be fine."

2. You tell her you appreciate her candor, and you will have to think about whether or not you want to pursue a friendship with her.

You say good-bye and congratulate yourself for valiantly pushing through your fear of rejection by asking her for a date.

The results may have changed, but *not* your response. You can be as proud of yourself for asking this woman for a date when she said, *"No,"* as when she said, *"Yes."* Why? Because the primary purpose behind these psychological and practical tools of meeting, greeting, and bonding is *not* to get you more dates (this is a secondary purpose) but to get you to *honor yourself* (by doing what you desire) rather than your fear (by doing nothing).

Whenever you honor yourself instead of your fear, you will always be proud of yourself, *regardless* of a woman's reaction.

Chapter Eight

Creating
Happy
Relationships

"Things do not change;
we change."
—Thoreau

This book is a blueprint for successful social connections with gay women. Although it is not a treatise on lesbian relationships, I believe the book would not be complete without a few useful hints on how to create happy relationships ... from the start.

MEET WOMEN FROM DESIRE, NOT DESPERATION

Many women believe, whether consciously or unconsciously, that they *must* find a lover to be happy. As a result, these women feel lonely, and their self-esteem is low. In their search to fill their emotional emptiness, they look outwardly for love and approval rather than looking inwardly. Often, they are not even aware that the energy they radiate is negative and insecure.

If you struggle with the problem of feeling incomplete without a lover, the only real solution is to love yourself more. Loving yourself lessens your need of love from others.

Seek love as an expression of and not a definition of self-esteem.

You must first love yourself before another woman can truly love you. In our society, unfortunately, we have been conditioned to believe the opposite: Find someone who loves you, and then you will love yourself. This thinking is dangerously faulty, and it is the reason why most of our relationships are dissatisfying. Expecting a relationship to heal a damaged sense of self is the reason for its failure.

Make a romantic relationship a delicious *part* of your life, not your whole life. A healthy, loving relationship is borne of *two* healthy, loving people. Whenever you love, you risk. But with a full life, if a relationship ends, it won't devastate you. You may feel sad, but you won't feel as though your whole world is falling apart. You know you will get through the pain, and eventually you will reach out, realizing that whatever happens you will be okay. This enlightenment gives you personal power to make choices from a place of *desire* rather than desperation.

So, to create healthy relationships, *love* yourself more and *need* others less. Design a full life by yourself, for yourself (refer to Chapter Two, "Self-Esteem"). Spend time with good friends and family. Volunteer for causes you care about. Spend self-nurturing time alone. Love your work or find work you love. Enjoy your hobbies ... do whatever makes you feel good.

When you aren't needy, you're more exciting to be around. You radiate positive and self-confident energy. Now *that* is attractive—and a great way to begin a relationship!

STOP FOCUSING ON FINDING THE RIGHT WOMAN; START FOCUSING ON *BEING* THE RIGHT WOMAN

Focusing on becoming your own Ms. Right is possibly the most important action you can take to having more fulfilling relationships. Begin by referring to your list of desirable qualities you want in a friend or lover (see Chapter Four, "Where the Women Are"). Ask yourself how many of these characteristics *you* possess. This is a crucial question because you must first *become* what you want in order to *find* who you want.

Our relationships are reflections of our deepest beliefs about ourselves; we unconsciously draw to ourselves exactly who we believe we *deserve*. When you cultivate in yourself the traits you seek in others, you will *believe* you are worthy of having a woman with these traits in your life. For example, if you *believe* you deserve sincere and loving women, you will *attract* sincere and loving women.

Start taking care of yourself, and watch how miraculously you start attracting more emotionally healthy and available women into your life.

AVOID THE "PERFECT WOMAN SYNDROME"

Some women create a mile-long list of requirements for the women they are willing to date. Before they even get to know another woman, they disqualify her because she doesn't match the list. They construct such an impossible test that the goddess herself would not pass it.

This "Perfect Woman Syndrome" is really fear of rejection in disguise. Many women demand perfection before getting emotionally involved because they are trying to protect themselves from getting hurt. If you never find someone who matches your requirements, you never have to *risk* being vulnerable. And, if you're never vulnerable, you can't be disappointed. This self-fulfilling prophecy is merely a form of self-sabotage.

In order to find a woman who is emotionally open, *you* must be emotionally open. Get rid of your unending list of pre-requisites; get to know someone one-on-one before summarily rejecting her. You may be amazed by the beautiful qualities you find when you take the time to get to know someone.

Chapter Nine

Final Thoughts

"That the birds of worry and care fly over your head, this you cannot change, but that they build nests in your hair, this you can prevent."
—Chinese Proverb

I want to leave you with some final thoughts on meeting women.

REJECT THE RULES

As little girls, we are taught rules of "proper" behavior.

Do any of these sound familiar?

"Act like a lady."
"Mind your own business."
"Don't talk to strangers."
"Don't draw attention to yourself."
"Be seen and not heard."
"Wait to be approached."
"It's better to be safe than sorry."

Traditionally, women have been socialized to be passive. This social conditioning is one of the reasons why so many of us stand around, waiting for someone else to make the first move. These childhood lessons *strangle* our adult social skills. Reject the rules! Discard these outmoded beliefs and trust yourself to act properly in social situations.

ASSUME THE BEST

Out of fear, you may not extend yourself to other

women. You may remain silent and tell yourself your standard defense:

"What if I ask her and she says, 'No'?"

Instead, tell yourself:

"What if I ask her and she says, 'Yes'?"

Rather than assuming the worst, assume the *best.* You may be pleasantly surprised. With risk, there exists the possibility of failure (rejection). But, there also exists the possibility of success (finding a new lover or friend).

THERE ARE NO STRANGERS

Remind yourself that we are all much more alike than we are different. We experience the same feelings—anger, joy, sadness, fear; we want to love and be loved; and we want acceptance, attention, and understanding. Concentrating on how alike we all are helps lessen our fear of each other. View other gay women not as strangers, but as friends we have not yet met.

FEAR OF MISUNDERSTANDING

Another fear that keeps us from reaching out to each other is the fear that our gesture of friendship will be misunderstood as a romantic proposal.

Some women ask me:
"What if she thinks I'm coming on to her when I only want to be friends?"

My answer is simple:
"So what?"

If your invitation is taken the wrong way, set her straight (excuse the expression) by explaining your intention:
"I'm sorry if you thought I was interested in dating you. That wasn't my intention. I'd like to get to know you as a friend."

If she doesn't want to have a platonic relationship with you, it serves both of you to find this out immediately.

YOU ARE ACCEPTED AT YOUR OWN SELF-APPRAISAL

Whenever you find yourself worried about what other women think of you, remind yourself that you are perceived by others as you perceive yourself. In other words, we are all accepted at our own self-appraisal.

If you don't like how other women behave toward you, stop, and ask yourself how you behave toward yourself. *Now* is the time to start treating yourself as you would like others to treat you.

LIKE ATTRACTS LIKE

If you're friendly toward a woman, she will be friendly toward you. If you're open with her, she will be open with you. Recall the universal law of attraction—like attracts like.

It's also true that if you're unfriendly toward a woman, she will be unfriendly toward you. It's as though we all unconsciously play the game, "follow the leader." Always behave toward a woman as you want her to behave toward you.

"I HATE THE BARS!"

I've heard many women say they, *"hate the bars,"* describing them as *"unfriendly"* and *"boring."* I believe the reason most of us dislike bars is that they can be very intimidating places to make contact with other women.

If you hate the bars because you can't stand being around smoke and alcohol, they are obviously the wrong place for *you*. But, if there is any chance you dislike bars out of fear of rejection, make sure you go to your nearest lesbian bar as soon as you complete this book. You'll have all the self-confidence strengthening tools you need to make social decisions from a place of *choice* rather than fear.

POSITIVE PREPARATION

Women are attracted to other women who are happy and having fun. Before going to a social event, mentally prepare to enjoy yourself:

1. Sit in a comfortable chair; close your eyes; take three deep breaths; and relax.

2. Practice "positive playback." In your mind, replay a wonderful experience you had meeting women. Remember how much fun you had and how happy you were.

3. Visualize yourself having a great time.

4. Remind yourself that the purpose of going out is to *have fun* meeting other women, not to find Ms. Right.

5. Assume women will like you. Your outer experiences reflect your inner beliefs. If you're convinced a woman will be friendly, you'll be open rather than defensive. And, most likely, she will return the kindness.

6. Decide to take a risk at the event by making the first move. Doing *nothing* is the biggest risk you can take. There may be

no risk of rejection, but there is also no reward of enjoyable contact.

7. Resolve to be your best self. When you let this part of you shine, you are best able to make emotionally fulfilling connections.

PUTTING IT ALL TOGETHER

It's easy for me to meet, greet, and bond with other gay women. Here's the reason—

I like lesbians.

That's it. Of course, there are some women I like more than others. But in general, I love our community. *Caring* about other women is the sina qua non of savvy socializing. It's effortless for me to show a woman that I genuinely care about her because I do.

How do *you* feel about our community?

If you don't feel as loving toward other gay women as you would like, learn to love yourself more. My own continual process of learning to love myself more has taught me something remarkable: The more I care about and appreciate *myself*, the more I care about and appreciate *other* women.

Meeting women for friendship or romance is a powerful self-improvement activity. It demands self-awareness and honesty, and it forces us to ask ourselves tough questions concerning what we really think about ourselves and our world.

Shyness is not a social skills problem; it is a self-esteem problem.

We are reluctant to approach other women when we don't feel good about ourselves. Making contact and talking with other women touches our deepest fears of failure.

Rejection does not cause low self-esteem; it merely exposes it.

Self-confidence and willingness to risk rejection are byproducts of self-love. Loving ourselves and others is the most important (and most challenging) work we will ever do. I believe it is *the* reason we are all here. I hope this book has provided some useful tools with which to do this essential work.

Thank you for the opportunity to share my thoughts with you. I would love to read your success stories. Please write me at:

Rhona Sacks c/o
SLOPE BOOKS™
Van Brunt Station
P.O. Box 150636
Brooklyn, NY 11215-0636

www.gaywoman.com

Index

Order Form

Phone orders: Call Toll Free: (888) GAYWOMAN
(orders only, please) Have your Visa
or Mastercard ready.

Fax orders: Fax Toll Free: (888) 355-8872
(orders only, please)

On-line orders: www.gaywoman.com

Mail orders: SLOPE BOOKS™
Van Brunt Station
P.O. Box 150636
Brooklyn, NY 11215-0636
(718) 832-8892

Please send me: ____ copy/copies of *The Art of Meeting Women: A Guide for Gay Women* @ $14.95 each.

Name _____

Address _____

City/State/Zip _____

Telephone _____

Shipping: $3.00 for the first book and $1.00 for
each additional book. (For Canadian
orders, please add an extra $2.00 for each
book.)

Sales Tax: Please add 8.25% sales tax to the total
amount due (including shipping) for
books shipped to New York addresses.

Payment: ____ Check (Canadian residents: please
pay by postal money order in U.S. funds.)
____ Mastercard ____ Visa

Card number: _____

Name on card: _____ Exp. date:___

Call or Fax Toll Free and Order Today

Order Form

Phone orders: Call Toll Free: (888) GAYWOMAN (orders only, please) Have your Visa or Mastercard ready.

Fax orders: Fax Toll Free: (888) 355-8872 (orders only, please)

On-line orders: www.gaywoman.com

Mail orders: SLOPE BOOKS™
Van Brunt Station
P.O. Box 150636
Brooklyn, NY 11215-0636
(718) 832-8892

Please send me: ____ copy/copies of *The Art of Meeting Women: A Guide for Gay Women* @ $14.95 each.

Name _____

Address _____

City/State/Zip _____

Telephone _____

Shipping: $3.00 for the first book and $1.00 for each additional book. (For Canadian orders, please add an extra $2.00 for each book.)

Sales Tax: Please add 8.25% sales tax to the total amount due (including shipping) for books shipped to New York addresses.

Payment: ____ Check (Canadian residents: please pay by postal money order in U.S. funds.) ____ Mastercard ____ Visa

Card number: _____

Name on card: _____ Exp. date:___

Call or Fax Toll Free and Order Today